FUNDAMENTALS
IN THE
FIRST SCHOOL

Plate 1 Boy, 4 yrs. 'Guardsman.'

FUNDAMENTALS
IN THE
FIRST SCHOOL

by

R. Bott   E. M. Hitchfield

M. P. Davies   J. E. L. Johnson

M. L. Glynne-Jones   J. R. Tamburrini

Chairman: M. Brearley
Froebel Institute College of Education

BASIL BLACKWELL · OXFORD

0 631 11840 3

© Basil Blackwell 1969
Reprinted 1970, 1972, 1974
Reprinted in Great Britain by
Compton Printing Ltd,
London and Aylesbury
Set by William Clowes and Sons, Limited
London, Beccles and Colchester
Bound by
The Kemp Hall Bindery
Oxford

Preface and Acknowledgments

This book was prepared by a group of people accustomed to working together. Our method of work was by group discussion, then individual writing, followed by group criticism and re-writing.

We acknowledge with appreciation and gratitude the many contributions from teachers, students and children, without which this book could not have been written.

List of Illustrations

Contents

CHAPTER 1

Introduction

WE ARE aiming at two things in preparing this little book for teachers and teachers in training. Firstly, to give an outline of the main considerations we feel should be taken into account when planning the education of young children and, secondly, to describe good practice as we have seen it, as examples of the application of these principles. We wish to make clear, at every stage, that these are *examples* and not methods. One of the reasons why new knowledge about children's learning is so slow to come into full operation in schools would seem to be the fatal habit of educators to trust too much to the apparatus, the gadget or the 'method' and by applying it indiscriminately, in what must then be many inappropriate situations, lose sight of the end for which it was designed. It would be false to suggest that this is behaviour peculiar to educators: architects, painters, actors, scientists, etc. are all open to the same error. The most economical place to attack the error, however, is clearly in the education of the young. The expectations and the habits of thought we fix in them are not lightly forgotten. We still await a full understanding of the growth of 'mind'. We need a psychologist who would trace and analyse our conceptual and other intellectual errors as Freud traced the genesis of emotional deviant behaviour. It is clear from the work of Piaget and Nathan Isaacs *et al.* that we have what might be termed a *cognitive* unconscious which is responsible for the strategies of thinking we employ and which must contain the source of much error. Meanwhile, much harm could be avoided by a training of teachers which puts all the emphasis on under-standing what one is doing and looking on all 'aids' as means to clearly envisaged ends and as likely, in themselves, to be ephemeral and contemporary as well as highly personal in use. It is not long since the writer saw a child, who had learnt to read fluently before he came to school, punished for not being able to sound out the phonic components of the words on a first reading card. It is easy not only to miss the wood for the trees but to overlook the fact that one ever had the wood in mind.

What, then, are these considerations? The first point to bear in mind is that a child has learnt in his own home and in his own way a great deal before he ever came to school. He has certainly learnt to move and to speak, though his level in both may differ greatly from other children of the same age.

He has learnt to look after at least some of his bodily needs, though his reliability in eating, eliminating, dressing and so on will also vary. He has learnt to love and hate, to laugh and cry, to assent and refuse, to pay attention and to refuse it. He has learnt to watch and to listen to items of interest to him. He has had an extensive acquaintance with a great variety of sounds, pleasant and unpleasant, many of which he can identify. He knows something of relationships and hierarchies and his place in them: something of the layout of his neighbourhood and perhaps of one or more others: he has some ideas of number and can perhaps recognize a few written words. He has observed a good deal about the sequence of events and is getting some sense of time both immediate and historical. He is beginning to understand the use of symbols. He knows, though he might not be able to explain it, that the name 'Pussy' is not identical with the animal itself, but 'stands for' it in speech, that his own name or the name on a newspaper or shop 'stands for' the object.

We must ask ourselves how he learnt these; in how far he was successful; if we have any filling-in to do; what would he be doing if he were not at school; what have we to add to this basic learning, and what new elements can we and do we wish to introduce? We must ask ourselves these questions and many more because school is a *planned* environment, planned by people professionally trained to do this. We can neither be content simply to let him go on growing as he has done up to now, nor can we justify cutting across this community pattern of learning. We plan an intervention: on what principles do we plan it?

If anything is certain about the learning process it is that one cannot miss out stages and hope to get a satisfactory end result. It is true that gifted children can shorten the process by needing less consolidation in some areas and that slow learning children may need some intermediary steps, but no one can proceed to stage two until stage one is completed, and this process is continuous and cumulative. Clearly, to teach children soundly we must take up their learning development where we find it, if we wish, as it were, to join the main stream. A period of careful observation, of talk with parents[1] about the early stages could often avoid the fatal confusion or almost equally fatal boredom that exists when children are credited with too much or too little previous knowledge.

The work of Piaget has thrown much light on this and will be referred to later, but there is much more to be learnt. The implications of the clearly marked stages of conceptual thought are beginning to be understood in some areas of knowledge and behaviour (e.g. mathematics, moral behaviour, early scientific ideas) but have so far been little touched on in connection with others.

What children have already learnt must be built on and appreciated if they are to begin to get a glimpse of their own learning powers and build up confidence in them. This is quite a different process from 'programmed learning' as it is usually understood, in which the operation starts from the breakdown of the subject matter in its mature adult form into

---

[1] If parents could be encouraged to keep simple records of their children's growth and development we could get many useful data from them. Not that this would be their only value. Froebel [see Bibliography, ref 31] was, perhaps, the first to point out an important 'side effect': 'Such a record would have a dual purpose. It would enlighten parents increasingly about their children, since they could explain their development in the light of earlier happenings and treat them in ways appropriate to their individual dispositions and character. Also children would discover later on that their parents had had a care for their unique personal life, their emotions and thoughts. Undoubtedly one of the mainsprings of a child's behaviour in all his searching and striving is the sort of care bestowed on his particular needs. He soon feels when his own individual self is the object of his parents' care and so comes to have confidence in them.'

the steps which logically should lead to mastery. Here the attention is concentrated on the results of the work and the approval attached exclusively to the end results. What we are suggesting involves paying attention to the learner and his own thought processes as well, so that we understand the nexus of the learner's own experience into which our teaching is to be incorporated and the level of thinking and conceptual skills he brings to it. The way a child has learnt before he comes to school is too often pushed aside as irrelevant. Unhappily we know that too many children reverse the process when they leave school. One of the faults of our early education has always been that we have not sufficiently studied what long-term results we have in mind. We wish in this book not to fall into this error but to consider how best to lay true foundations so that the knowledge acquired in these early years may prove to be active and functional in the life of the individual. Society is lavish in its criticism of the lack of responsibility, the escape from reality, the dislike of work, etc. shown by many teenagers. Has their early education contributed to this? Can educators plan for a different result?

Another basic consideration when we are planning our primary education must be the whole subject of 'motivation'. Everyone knows in his own life and work to what extent the amount of energy available for what we have to do is dependent on the strength of our motives. Because young children have not developed all the possible motives for efforts, both those that are worthy and those that are not: because they are untouched by ambition: because they are unaware of the extent to which the comfort and satisfaction of their lives will depend on qualifications, etc. and because no idea of responsibility for others or for disseminating such truth as one sees has yet arisen, we have tended in the past to provide artificial semblances of these in 'position in class', house points, prizes, a bicycle for passing 11 + and so on. Should we not seek to find the true purposes in the stage of early childhood and therefore the sources of energy?

Observation of young children can show some unmistakable sources. First there is the physical need of the growing organism for frequent and varied movement and the allied psychological need to explore the possibilities of his own physical achievements. Without this, it is clear that a growing child could not develop the power and control that keeps him safe. (This is at the core of all accident prevention.) The writer once saw a four-year-old child, well grown and well nourished, who had been tied in a chair for two years by a baby farmer. When the child was rescued she could neither walk nor speak and appeared mentally defective. She went rapidly through all the stages of development she had missed with a kind of desperate energy which pointed to the depth of her need, both physical and psychological, for natural activity. Children in a too formally run school show this frenzy as they rush into the playground, and there, if there is no suitable opportunity for all the climbing, jumping, swinging, etc. that their minds and bodies need, they have recourse to 'rough behaviour', destructiveness or meaningless and mindless ritual.

Curiosity as a source of energy can hardly be considered separately. It is the whole outward thrust of the organism which really means its life. Everything in a child's environment can be an object of intense curiosity to him and everything contains within it something from which he can learn. The teacher's part in this is a complex one and will be more fully explored later, but briefly it consists in deepening that interest into knowledge. This is a quite different process from giving 'a little learning'. This knowledge cannot be developed in a barren classroom. Children must bring their outside life into the classroom to get help in organizing it into a conceptual framework. This is part of the alternating cycle between 'actuality' and thought which constitutes our cognitive and affective build up (see Chapter 9). As children see so many (by comparison with adults) 'new' objects and meet with so many new facets of behaviour, they are faced with the constant and demanding need to adapt to these and to build up the framework of expectations which enables us to interpret our world. This framework or structure has its main lines laid down in the first seven or eight years of life.

When children bring objects or experiences to the classroom the teacher's part is to supply language, ask questions, provide further stimulus or material and to lift the whole activity on to a more conscious level. A conversation with a four-year-old will serve as an illustration:

'I've been watching Parsley the Lion, daddy.'
'Have you?'
'Yes—it's the same as Auntie Parsley.'
'Well, it's the same name, it isn't the *same* is it?'
'Oh no—Auntie Parsley's a lady, Parsley the Lion is a man.'
'Oh he's a man, is he?'
'Well—no—anyway he's a man lion!'

Teaching is a cultural task and our business is to gear these natural curiosities and interests to the traditional skills which the culture has built up and valued. There is no literal suggestion here that the children must rediscover these skills, but that a child should first discover the need for them so that we have the energy of his willingness on our side. The waste of spirit, on both sides, involved in unwilling learning is known by every teacher, though its forms and causes are not always recognized.[1]

A third large source of energy is connected with our lives as emotional and social beings. The need for the love and appreciation of adults and of other children, whatever its origin, is a motive which can become easily exploited. It may well be that it becomes twisted so easily because the urgency of the need is such that in one form or another it must be obtained without delay. The way we deal with this depends on our own philosophy of life. If we do genuinely believe in the unique value of every human being, we cannot suffer a child in our classroom who is deprived of this basic need of a 'whole' life. It is often the child who has for some reason failed to get the necessary love and appreciation of his parents who begins a failing life in school at five years old or earlier. The teacher must have available a deep concern for him, must help him to good relationships with other children and adults and must, too, in every possible way influence the parents concerned to modify, however slightly, their attitude. The soundest way, it would

[1] 'How much time and labour, and impatience, and compulsion on the part of the teacher, and dislike and fretting, and hatred on the part of the pupil might be saved, if instructors would permit children to get knowledge *in* school in the same manner that Nature teaches *out* of it.' J. Orville Taylor (1854), quoted in *Teaching to Read Historically Considered*. (Mitford M. Mathews 1966.)

seem, lies in so observing a child that we are enabled to discover a genuine strength or potential talent and in helping him in every way to develop this, thus putting it in his power to gain approval on legitimate grounds.

A class, well known to the writer, containing children of very varied abilities has been so well educated by a gifted teacher over a three-year period, that every child is supported by the teacher's knowledge of him, his strengths and his weaknesses and is well known by his companions in the same fashion. There is much evidence in this class that children's appreciation of each other's knowledge, skills and feelings provides a springboard for much satisfying extension of power in each child. Their 'performance' reaches a level far higher than one could expect from their measured IQs. Just as within a street, a club, a business or a university, people function at very different levels, so we should expect this within each group of children. Much of the unreal and unrealistic comparing of children within a group rises from some theoretical postulate of exact levels and standards appropriate to each age. This is unreal because people are virtually unmeasurable,[1] and unrealistic since it does not in any way correspond to life as they will live it afterwards.

The 'considerations' discussed so far refer to conditions within which the main work of the school can best be carried out. The main work of the school is surely the fostering and developing of mental life, enabling children to experience more fully and consciously all that life has to offer. This large overall aim is to be achieved by an infinity of small steps. The material we provide can seldom be thought of as an end in itself but rather as a means through which effective thinking and feeling are fostered. It is important, for instance, that a child should

---

[1] We have many false and misleading instruments of measurement. The value of tests of reading and arithmetic, for instance, is great and has marked some real steps forward in our understanding but their crudity can easily be overlooked. It would be difficult to find two seven-year-olds, say, with exactly the same ability in reading. They might each reach the same point on a word recognition test or gain the same marks on a comprehension one but the development of their capacity to read may be at very different stages. The 'fringe' words that are *not* tested might show a power in one that is absent in the other: the comprehension exercise achieved by one might represent the limit of his capacity and by the other might signify its beginning.

learn to read for extrinsic and intrinsic reasons. He must satisfy himself, his parents and society that he can achieve the common cultural level of literacy. If this were all, however (and it *is* sometimes all), we should have missed the best opportunity of making him free of the thoughts and ideas of others and of enriching his own life with them. Of course he needs to be able to read for much of the practical running of his life, but we are aiming, too, at communication at a much higher level. It is this second aim that determines the way we teach reading and guides the selection of books for the primary school, as it should for all other sections of the school.

Building up the power to think clearly and effectively should be the constant aim of our teaching. It cannot be said too often that the different ways of thinking need specific exercise: we cannot assume that remembering alone, however effective it can become, will provide all the thinking skills we need. In its largest sense, of course, remembering is the basis of all other learning: we cannot learn, for instance, to 'estimate' unless we have memories of earlier experience, but these are memories of *our* experience and too much 'memory work' in school has been of quite another kind. Unless the ideas are fully understood any teaching of new mathematics or any other subject can fall into this error.

The following sequence occurred in a recent T.V. programme on 'new mathematics'. 'How many numerical operations would you think a computer could do in a minute?' Silence. The children had absolutely no basis of experience on which to estimate. The teacher pressed further: 'Would you say 10? or 100? or more?' The children, obeying the inflexion in her voice, answered 'more'. They had not estimated, they had echoed. Examples will be given in other chapters of the development of the power to analyse and synthesize, to make judgments and to estimate, to solve problems, to follow logical sequences of thought, to make and test hypotheses.

The 'feeling' side of our mental life equally needs cultivation: means of communication through language and the arts provide for the expression, use and control of feeling and response. The arts and sciences have here a dual role in that they give the opportunity for defining and understanding the self and for entering into the lives and experiences of others, a cycle corresponding to that described in the cognitive field.

It is clear that a complex of development such as has been described cannot be distilled into a set of 'lessons', nor can it be left to 'happen' even in a well-furnished school. The genesis of it all is the self-chosen activity which arises as the result of a child's own response to a set of circumstances. The wise teacher joins this forward thrust and helps a child to define, fix and organize his responses, genuinely preparing for more structured approaches in later work. This can be clearly seen in every area of work we have studied: a child's natural movements of elation or anger can be isolated and repeated with intention to bring about planned effects: a child's own vocalization can be matched to an instrument or recorded on paper and therefore can be 'fixed' and repeated for a purpose. So it can be with painting, reading, number, science and the rest. Even many early experiences of moral behaviour may be developed in this way. A child's spontaneous generosity or control of himself can form the basis of his learning. The initiative comes from the children, the referral to the developed systems is done by the adult, parent or teacher. This should be done, of course, without labouring too many points. The objective is not tied to these specific points but is a more global one: to set up the mental habits of structured thinking.

The development of knowledge is personal, the younger the child the less 'public' his learning can be. It is interesting to note that a group of children who have a common core of activities experienced together can come to the point of discovering in practice that knowledge is common. By virtue of much shared experience they can, at times, learn together but still for the most part of the time side by side. There is an analogy here with their social development. Individual play in the baby, fostered and ministered to by parents, is followed by two children playing side by side until their individual experiences find a common ground and then they combine (and oppose!) forces, at first for very short periods.

There are, of course, many experiences that first school children can enjoy profitably together. The feeling in a group of young children listening to a story is a mysterious phenomenon: mysterious, because they will often listen absorbed to what is a poor effort judged on objective standards. It may be that, like the tired business man, they want a rest from being themselves (and one should not underrate the tremendous achievements of the first eight years of life when a child is very literally making up his own mind and self) or that at a higher level they are seeking, however unconsciously, to enlarge their sympathies and understanding like the more serious theatre-goer or reader. The same applies to listening to music and poetry: there is a group experience as well as the individual one. There is, too, a process of 'validation' going on when the children discover that others see, hear, think and feel many of the same things as they do themselves.

In all *this* kind of 'class teaching' the children can respond, each at his own level. This is very different from asking a group to follow a logical series of steps together, in which failure to understand one involves failure in the whole and children are then forced back on to an attempt to recapture the *words* instead of reliving the understanding.

There are many more subtle ways in which children in-fluence the personal growth or learning in each other. A child brought the unlikely word 'serendipity' into the class because he had heard it discussed on T.V. This group of eight-year-olds had had an interest in words fostered in them by constant appropriate reference. They liked the sound of the word in spite of its difficulty and doubtless things 'happening by happy chance' are more frequent in the lives of children, innocent of so many probabilities, than in adults and therefore the idea was not difficult in itself. The word was discussed, and there it might have ended if someone had not found it in a library book. 'I found John's word!' not only gave significance to John but in his mind and that of many others, the word became 'real' and, while the craze lasted, much used.

This incident has been described in detail, because the unusualness of the word made its progress easy to trace—just as one can trace the activity of a single cell by staining it to distinguish it from the others. This must be a prototype of one of the many ways our complex of meaning and language is built up. The creative task is the individual's but the sources are many. The complexity of the task can be glimpsed by extension forward and outward.[1]

The need to have long-term results in mind has already been mentioned. What are the characteristics of 'a good thinker'? Although the proportion of the different thinking abilities will vary according to the nature of the problem under consideration, these characteristics can be described in general terms.

The first to be considered is confidence. A child who approaches any problem with confidence in his own ability to solve it brings a special kind of energy or heightened emotional tone to the task, which is likely to be productive. There can, of course, be over-confidence, but this is rarer than the timidity and apathy which follows too many unsuccessful attempts. This confident attitude, if it is properly based on the kind of self-knowledge gained by previous success, encourages a child to persist after several false starts because he has had reason to believe from the past that effort will bring a solution.

The chapter on science refers to the fact that scientific knowledge grows by a process of the verification or otherwise of expectations, which are determined by action. A child who has approached learning in this spirit is at the ready for activity, can see failure as a negative result from which one can learn and can summon up the mental energy for further trial. To see 'failure' in this light as part of the process of gaining knowledge rather than its *opposite* is surely one of the aspects of scientific thinking we should do well to consider.

'Must learn to concentrate more' has appeared on nearly everyone's school report at some time. Such a remark postulates a general power of concentrating regardless of the material: it

---

[1] Some idea of the complexity of the task may be conveyed by the following extract from *The Memory System of the Brain* by J. Z. Young: 'The need for a logical strategy is imposed on us by the fact that the brain is a multi-channel system, with numerous parts of very small size. There are probably at least 10,000 synaptic points on one large cortical neuron (perhaps many more). How many of these would be altered when an animal has learned? Would they all change at once? Would some have been changed by previous learning? Worse still, there must be thousands of synaptic vesicles in a single presynaptic terminal. If learning consists in the production of a flood of inhibitory or excitatory transmitters, what changes, if any, should we expect to see in the vesicles?'

may well be that people do differ radically from each other in the general level of their concentration but this is an extremely complex matter to investigate in any 'real' situation. Those who hope to test it by 'proof reading' and other similar tests are measuring something, undoubtedly, and even something that it is useful to investigate, but common observation tells us that this is only part of the matter. Since as yet we do not know how much of this ability is innate or genetically influenced, we should do well to consider it at any rate as modifiable and educable. The importance to the individual of the issue he is investigating seems to play a larger part than any general ability. How do we foster this power to absorb oneself in a task? How does this differ from the perseveration of the mentally inert child? This question awaits much research but meantime careful recording of children's responses to different material will tell us much. One way of approach is to note those materials which call forth the longest concentration span at various ages and provide fully for these. The experience of concentrating in itself is of value and the teacher, who by a timely provision of a new piece of material or a comment or a question, can prolong the time given to one topic by thus deepening it, may well be making an important contribution to the development of concentration. To say that the *experience* of concentration is of value needs some amplification. A child who is held to a task by the concentration of the teacher may not be having this experience at all. Again if the experience does not bring satisfaction it will not be readily repeated. This satisfaction can be of many kinds. The primary satisfaction of the successful completion of a task is the most obvious, though this in itself is not always simple. A child may well need his success made explicit: his achievement may need the summing up of the adult: partial success sometimes needs to be defined to indicate what has yet to be done. A homely example might be that of a seven-year-old child who has written a letter to request permission for the class to visit some place of interest. This seemingly simple operation can prove a task requiring great concentration since it involves a precision and clarity of intent not usually called for from children for whom all arrangements of this kind are commonly provided at home. Moreover, this is called for at the same time as he has to give a high level of

conscious attention to the act of writing, spelling and arrangement. He brings the letter to the teacher: it is likely to be imperfect and she must exercise swift judgment on how to receive
it. One thing is clear, the achievement must be appreciated and
acknowledged if we wish the child to return willingly and con-
fidently to repair the omissions, etc. The teacher who meets
the situation with immediate disparagement takes away this
willingness and confidence, and impairs the child's power of
learning. It is also (but not equally so, I suggest), damaging
to overpraise or to accept (except for some good reason) a
poor level of effort. What we wish to do is to develop the power
of self-criticism. On the basis of reasonably successful outcomes
from his concentrating he should learn to tolerate criticism.

The habit of estimating, used so frequently in everyday life,
is often left to look after itself. Some problems call for a swift
summing up of the situation, an estimate or analysis into
categories which can bring economy in work. Children who
are trained to estimate, not in the sense of a wild guess, but by
building up some frames of reference can develop a high degree
of skill within appropriate limits. Those adults who are used to
estimating in connection with their work have usually a number
of personally acquired prototypes which they use as units, e.g.
the usual height or width of a door, the length of a cricket
pitch, their own height, weight etc. If these are acquired early
they can function very accurately. 'I should think we need two
of those pieces of wood to make the frame long enough' needs
the later comment, 'We *thought* we needed two but found we
needed two and a half when we measured', to round off this
piece of learning, and later even, 'I *always* think we need less
than we do'.

A mental habit of synthesizing and seeking analogies is
another characteristic of 'a good thinker' which needs attention
and training. It can, of course, be a fruitful source of error and
children should be encouraged from the beginning to be
rigorous with themselves in any matching activity they indulge
in. The four-year-old who remarked that the caravan was the
same colour but not the same shape as grandpa's was helping
himself by putting into words the limitation he perceived. The
teacher's job here is often to ask the question which will challenge the too hasty assumption.

The cultivation and use of imagination is not easily defined. We often speak of it and may be meaning anything from the fairies at the bottom of the garden to the most creative level of thinking. It must, at least, have something to do with the formation of images. The appearance of the classroom, the level and variety of the presentation, the ordering of the materials within it, the recognition of tactile, olfactory and auditory images as well as visual ones and the struggle for its accurate description, representation and interpretation must play their parts in the building up of the capacity to use imagination.

The provision of books, stories, poems, pictures, music, fabrics, etc. is, of course, a very personal matter. One dreads the appearance of 'kits' for these things. They must surely be introduced as part of the personal relationship between the children and the teacher and knit into the complex of activities current in the school. These will naturally involve much reference to the music, art and literature from the past but it has often been observed that young children can respond to the modern idiom in any medium with greater ease often than their elders. They are the people for whom it is appropriate.

Another aspect of the use of the imagination is in personal relationships. Here the incidental reference in a story, for instance, 'What would you have done?', 'How do you think his mother felt when he ran away?', etc. can help that difficult shift from the purely personal view of events which some people, it seems, never make. Dramatic work and make-believe play is the natural exercise of this. The literal putting of yourself in another's place and the discussion of thoughts, feelings and motives gives scope for natural intrinsic development at the child's own level rather than presenting him with an artefact of aphorisms or pious statements which can remain disastrously unconnected with action.

Much will be said during the following chapters on the subject of communication. The development of language skills in particular can be influenced directly by the teacher. The work of Luria, Bernstein *et al.* has reinforced our belief in the importance of precision, variety and complexity of language in the development of thinking and in the degree to which educational opportunity can be taken.

Many children come from homes where the language background is poor. In the past, teachers who recognized this as a disability tried to fill in this inadequacy with vocabulary exercises, etc. This was indeed better than nothing but could not possibly take the place of the *organic* growth of language arising in experiences which provoke the need for new words for their definition. Many children from underprivileged homes have very few nouns, the few pronouns doing duty for most objects and people. This means that the finer shades of discrimination shown by the use of a variety of adjectives is not called for and often thus not developed. The almost exclusive use of the present tense and the very limited use of clauses keeps the children's speech at a level which makes it very difficult for them to read the material written for them by adults at a very different cultural level. One can find books written for children of this age which contain sentences of forty or more words. This presents a formidable problem to a child whose average sentence length is four words. Children must learn to think and speak in sentences which bear some relationship to those we ask them to read if we look on reading as a means of extending knowledge and experience.

A teacher has day-long opportunities of arousing an interest in words, in using and helping children to use the appropriate technical terms and, by the age of eight certainly, laying the foundation of an interest in derivations which can illuminate understanding for the rest of life. A teacher must feed in much of this and *listen for the feedback*. It is the extent to which these words and structures genuinely function in the children's speech and writing that determines her success or failure.

In the following chapters will be found descriptions of how these general ideas can be applied to the many areas of experience commonly found in the infants' school under the names of music, movement, science, number, English, painting and 'moral code'. These are not thought of in isolation from each other but as interlocking and interacting. They are present, *as subject matter*, mainly in the teacher's mind, and they must *be* present. It is important that the continued study by the teacher in order to keep his own knowledge up to date and to preserve his own satisfaction in learning should be regarded as an essential ingredient of 'modern methods'.

We have tried to demonstrate that the same principles are being discussed whatever the material, at the same time showing how each area of experience may call more heavily on some aspects of human behaviour than on others, as indicated by the subtitles of the chapter headings. In each area we have tried to show how we can ensure continuity of learning from the massive volume of experience a child had in his first years of life before he ever came to school.

We have not attempted to touch on all areas of life in the first school, the importance of full co-operation with parents, the need for live contacts with the neighbourhood, the methods of school or class organization, but have been mainly concerned with the process of learning and the principles on which we base our teaching.

We have provided a selected bibliography which will give the background of the ideas expressed.

CHAPTER 2

Science: Expectations, Conjectures and Validations

HUMAN learning is a process of building up an internal model of the world. This is a personal experience: but a new-born child has no store of personal experiences upon which to build. There is certainly evidence that he has virtually seen nothing, tasted nothing, heard nothing, smelled nothing and felt nothing. Thus the world has no coherence for him. At birth the child cannot even be taught, and so has to learn for himself. At first this learning will be derived from chance events, and then from his own experiments. It will be characterized by the relation of his own actions to external events, by which he gradually differentiates patterns of behaviour through which he interprets the world. In so doing, the young baby manifests *purpose*. Although he may explore at random, he is beginning to search for what has happened before and purpose gives a direction to search. However, not all particular, organized sensitivities to the environment are learnt from experience. For example, as a bird inherits in its genetic endowment the ability to build nests, so a baby is equipped with the sucking reflex.

In this technological age, much of our adult information about the world is achieved through the use of technical and scientific apparatus. However delicate and complex this is the scientific investigator shares with all of us the fact that, in the end, what he records enters his mind directly through his senses. Whether it is an ordinary everyday happening, or an investigation conducted with the use of scientific instruments, e.g. a microscope, a galvanometer or an X-ray spectrometer, ultimately the data are interpreted after passing through one or more of our five senses.

But what the senses report does not have meaning in itself, for each message is piecemeal and unstructured. As Bronowski [8] [1] points out, we build up a model of the world only as we learn to link one message with another, to relate what the ear hears with what the hand touches and the eye sees. Smells, tastes, visual patterns, sounds and tactile events are differentiated and organized into a unified whole. Both the ordinary human being and the scientist share similar experiences in this way. The discoveries of science are not there to be picked up. They come into being only by an activity enacted between the scientist and his selected environment. In an analogous manner, the child has to find reality for himself, by building up from simple to more complex experiences.

By learning to co-ordinate his actions, particularly visual and grasping ones, the young child invents space for himself. Like scientists, children make their discoveries through creative activity. They do not record just what they see: they *experiment*. Experimentation is the means by which scientific theories are improved and modified. Similarly a child improves his interpretation of the world. As the child grows, and takes more and more things into account, so the interpretation is refined and elaborated.

A further major discovery by the child is that of the permanent existence of objects [43]. Once a child has learned that even when an object is out of sight it is still somewhere, he starts a new stage in mental awareness. Such a child is beginning to separate the world from himself. Up to this point he has been learning to manipulate objects with his hands and mouth: now he can start to manipulate them in thought. The child begins to be aware of the world as consisting of things and people, of which he is one. He has moved into a world of imagination and reason. This is a basic step, for when the child has learned to be aware of the existence of something which has been put out of sight, out of the immediate field of the senses, thought rests upon the formation of images. Thought and imagination therefore are inseparable.

[1] The figures in square brackets refer to the Select Bibliography at the end of the book.

The unexpected event frequently stimulates intellectual comment. No doubt the child whose illustration is reproduced below, brought to bear earlier fruitful experiences and concepts to achieve such startlingly vivid discrimination.

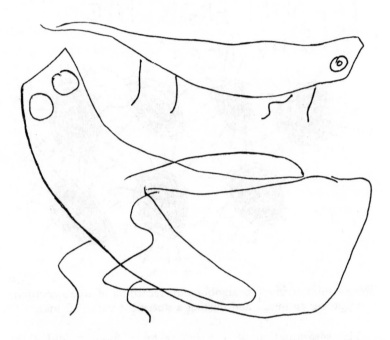

An owl eating a rat: seen in a car's headlamp, by a 3½-year-old.

A child comes to school equipped in some measure with an imaginative curiosity about the world around him. This chapter is concerned with how we, as teachers and educators, help him to order his experiences into a rational unity. Young children should find in the schools a nurturing influence for their natural curiosity. It is to be expected that many of their investigations will be transitory and fleeting, for they are seeking merely to answer specific questions. But as they build up understanding of relationships, so they begin to search for more general statements.

Here we have an example by a six-year-old boy recording a piece of exploratory behaviour.

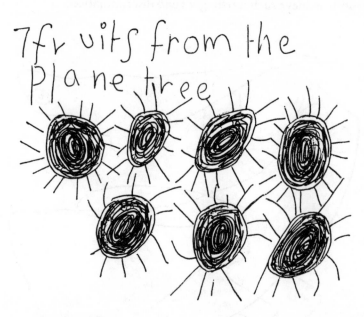

Six-year-old: a simple straightforward recording of an observation, reproducing an image and making a statement about his find.

The reproduction of a painting by a five-year-old child illustrates the inspiration of a sprig of spring larch, resulting in acute observation. The colours that the child used in this painting are indicated by appropriate labelling.

Searching strategies are characteristic, too, of scientific investigations. This is strictly in the tradition of Francis Bacon (1561–1626). His contention was that the natural world is not going to reveal its qualities to a passive observer. Nature has to be stirred up, as it were, and experiences have to be devised. Such contrived events are what Bacon would term experiments. It is important to note that this view of the experiment is merely that of *adding* to the number of natural events, though in circumstances where we are on the look out for what is happening. It is this sort of experiment that the teacher is providing

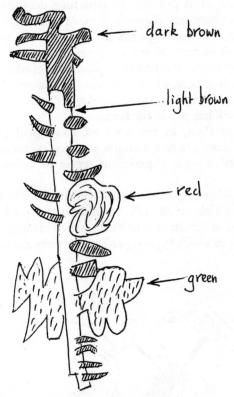

Five-year-old: Spring larch

for, for instance, when various materials are offered in the water trough for testing floating and sinking properties. This is a view of the role of the experiment distinct from that where a situation is contrived to test a theory or hypothesis. This latter role of the experiment is the more difficult, for it does not attempt just to answer questions of *how?*, and to classify events but seeks to satisfy questions of *why?*. This is a much more difficult procedure, for it involves a critical process based upon certain logical criteria, i.e. if such and such a theory is correct, then it must follow that such and such an event must take place, given the required circumstances. Moreover, this is more than just a *predictive* process, for theory includes an imaginative explanation and understanding of what is.

By contrast, it is possible to structure detailed predictive statements without any theoretical explanations for the events. For example, Toulmin [50 pp. 27–30] cites the Babylonians, with their calculations about astronomical events. They could forecast quite easily, but had no explanation of what caused the movements. It is true, of course, that in a general sense they held a theory—that of natural regularity: what has happened in the past will happen in the future.

Experiment then, in the sense of theoretical justification, attempts to answer *why* questions, to offer explanation, whilst in the Baconian sense experiment serves to answer only *how* questions.

The two following examples of children's attempts at the experiment which seeks only to add to the pool of natural events consist of drawn and written records of classroom miniature gardens, in which typical garden creatures are kept.

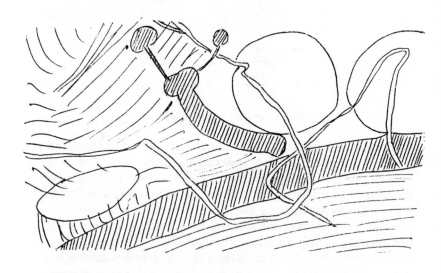

Seven-year-old girl: 'There is a stone a snail a bathing pool grass Roots and all the orange liens are were the snail Has Been There is one very Long stick that Reaches to the pond and to the stone.'

The second example is more detailed and relational in its account of the creature's activities.

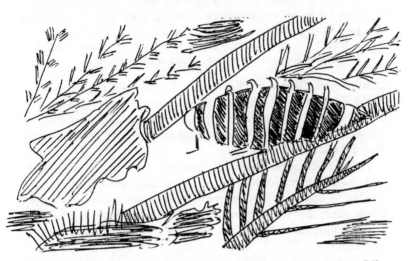

Seven-year-old girl: 'The wood lice like wood to be wet they Like the stones to Be wet too they like grass to be wet they go under the stones they go up trees. then they go Down trees to the mud under the stones they go to sleep.'

An imaginative teacher will take advantage of interesting occurrences that capture individual children's attention. Here are some notes taken from a teacher's daily account. It concerned initially a boy of five years.

> Discovered frost still in patches on the ground. We picked up a leaf that was clearly covered and took it inside.
> Examined frost particles with a magnifying glass that I had provided in the classroom. Began to see them melt.
> 'Miss, it's getting wet. It's all going.'
> 'Where is it going?'
> 'Inside there!' (pointing to the leaf)
> He went and fetched some more leaves and watched the frost melting with the heat. Very exciting! A little later, when the leaves were only slightly damp he was touching them again.
> 'It's sticky, Miss, not wet.'
> 'Where is all the water going?'
> 'Inside there!'

Talked about this a great deal. As yet imperfect understanding of what went on as the frost melted, but knows why
it melted. However, basis laid for further extension. Introduced this as discussion later in the morning. J. S. thought that
Jack Frost put it there during the night.

Other kinds of frozen water were talked about, and I.S.
mentioned the pond freezing over in cold weather.

Subsequently the teacher decided to extend the experience
of the frost melting and provided some ice cubes. These were
placed around the room in various containers and the following
questions were posed: What makes them melt? How long do
they take to melt?

From a scientific point of view the experiment was crude
and was further limited by the fact that the children were
unable to measure time in minutes. But they were fascinated
particularly by the sequential order of melting: (1) held in
hand, (2) on radiator, (3) ice contained in a clay vessel and (4)
ice outside.

Much discussion—noticed water mixed with clay, becoming
coloured by it—lots of water coming from cubes—liquids from
solids.

The imagination frequently brings together the most in-
congruous of relationships. There was great argument one
afternoon between some five- and six-year-old children as to
the relative strengths of an elephant and an octopus.

P. Elephant is bigger.
T. An octopus has more legs.
I. So he could strangle an elephant easily.
J. But an elephant has tusks which are sharp: that would stop
him.

Following a discussion on the possible needs of plants, two
seven-year-old boys put a tin over a plant. They had very
little idea of what might happen but had an expectation that
the plants would die if they were excluded from the light, or
were not watered.

In considering the function of science in the classroom, we
must decide initially what we mean when we use the term

'science'. The popular notion is that of a large collection of facts carefully classified and structured, a kind of reservoir of technical know-how. This we might use firstly, in an instrumental way, to solve practical problems and secondly as a source of explanation which reveals to us the nature of the world. From the first point of view we would regard the telephone directory as a fragment of science. But this seems to be far too restrictive a notion. Science, it is true, includes a body of knowledge, but in appreciating its full meaning, it is necessary to include the *methods* by which such knowledge is acquired. When we come to do this we are involved in considering the activities of scientists.

It would seem that knowledge is derived, at least in part, from experience, but no statement by a single person reporting an experience can be incorporated into scientific knowledge, no matter how strong the conviction. It has to undergo a kind of inter-subjective scrutiny. That is to say, it has to be confirmed by others using agreed methods of testing. Only in this way can it be said that the data is objective, and may become incorporated into the body of knowledge. This inter-subjective requirement shows us that the growth of scientific knowledge is a social act. The history of science is set in the solving of human practical problems: an intellectual effort embedded in the changing needs of mankind. Similarly, the growth of understanding by children in the natural scene around them, arises out of practical problems which the teacher has the responsibility of drawing to the children's attention.

In the adult world of science, individuals contribute, but only within a social context. In a classroom providing opportunities for experiment, children will arrive at tentative conclusions and should be encouraged to submit them to the scrutiny of group discussions. As indicated earlier, the judgment is not just on the *results* of experiments, but also upon the *method*. It is the examination of the means by which a statement has been derived that determines whether it is acceptable. One important notion to get across to young children is whether an observation is invariant to individuals, e.g. 'Do you think if John tried our floating and sinking experiment it would happen in a similar way for him?'

Thus only after children have come to see that things behave consistently from individual to individual, providing other conditions are similar, can they challenge a claim on the grounds that the method of acquiring the result is as much a part of the discovery as the so-called discovery itself.

Science is not the only social activity that demands an inter-subjective agreement. Art, too, requires some measure of acceptance. Both being social activities, they need to gain this acceptance before they can be incorporated within the body of artistic or scientific expression. An important distinction between the two, however, is that a work of art is appraised as a finished product—for example, a novel, a painting or a piece of sculpture. Although we may be interested for other reasons in the processes that led up to the finished piece of artistic work, this in no way affects the evaluation of it as a work of art. But a scientific statement, as distinct from an artistic one, requires not only that we scrutinize it as the result of a method, but also that we scrutinize and make a judgment upon the method as well.

A work of science must not only provide a conclusion, but also the means by which it was reached. The statement that there are invisible elephants living on Mars would never gain acceptance scientifically, without an accompanying explanation of how this remarkable conclusion was reached. The method of acquiring the result is bound up with the discovery. It is important to appreciate, therefore, that the criterion of general assent has to be understood in this broader sense. The criterion for science is more social than individual, while the artistic world is by its very nature, less unified.

Yet from the point of view of the individual effort of the artist or scientist, there is little difference in the manner of handling their respective problems. Both manifest imagination or inspiration. With the research worker in the laboratory this is most obvious: before he decides the detailed nature of his test, he has already jumped ahead of his evidence. For any particular test he sets up is determined solely by the expected result he seeks. Thus verification waits upon action; and the kind of action is determined by expectations. The term 'expectations' is not to be understood as prior knowledge of results, for if this were so there would be no point in setting up the test. An expectation is a derivative from a point of view about a task in hand. The point of view determines what we observe, and we make a discriminatory forecast. Objects can be classified, and can become similar or dissimilar only in this way, by being related to needs and interests. This applies to the inquiring child as well as to the scientist.

In the following example of six-year-old children discussing the behaviour of air coming out of a balloon, we can see how attempts at prediction are bound up with trying to render the behaviour of the balloon intelligible. This latter requirement is achieved by putting forward explanation: it is an attempt at understanding.

> G. brought a balloon to school, which he blew up partially, and then let go so that it flew round the room. Asked what had happened, one of the children said that the air had come out. The movement of the balloon was demonstrated again.
> 'Can you tell me why it's moving away?'
> 'Is it rather like a magnet? The balloon is going along after the air. The air is coming out, and the balloon is following like a magnet,' said N.
> J. 'It's the pressure. Only a little bit of air can come out, so it's moving along.'
> The children watched again, and gradually N. saw that the balloon went in the opposite direction from the way the opening was facing. J. noted the curved route of the balloon, and he stationed himself where he thought the balloon would end up.

What the human being, and therefore the child, picks out in his observations in attempting to make sense of the world, is determined by the special problem under investigation and his frame of reference or horizon of expectations. Observation then, as Karl Popper [45 pp. 46–47] points out, is always selective. It requires a chosen object, a definite task, an interest, a point of view, a problem. Moreover, the description of an observation presupposes a descriptive language, with words designating properties. It presupposes similarities, differences and classification. These in their turn presuppose interests, points of view and problems.

The particular selectivity of observation is drawn attention to by Caws [11 pp. 47, 49]. If perception consists in what and how a man sees, feels, hears, smells and tastes, then observation is a special form of perception. The observer concentrates on particular phenomena with a view to describing them by means of care-fully defined class terms, so that they can form the starting points for generating theories. Further, an experiment is an artificial device for putting the observer in a favourable position with respect to nature: a contrivance to arrange events where they can be seen. The science student brings to his activity his sensory apparatus, ordinary language habits and some understanding of the appropriate standard language. Left entirely to themselves, science students would recapitulate to some degree, the history of science. Learning is accelerated and structured in a logical hierarchy if the material to be studied is presented in a heuristic way and with students adequately prepared. New concepts can be introduced in the appropriate places for the structuring of new definitions, rather than in the order in which they were originally discovered.

At the primary school stage we are introducing science for its educative value rather than its material utility. We are not aiming necessarily to produce scientists or to make 'new' discoveries. We are concerned not so much that children should arrive at the same results as highly trained scientists as to see that they draw conclusions from their own information in a rational way. Children will make statements which they can put to the test. They will ask questions and can be encouraged to ask questions which are best answered by their own observations and experiments.

Observation, then, plays an important part in the activity. Everyone observes, but most people with only limited accuracy. It is a skill born of interest, training, practice and evaluation. Awareness has to be directed to those features which concern the problem in hand and this is what makes demands on the teacher's skill. For example, children will watch a blue tit at a bird table and show pleasurable excitement at its antics. Yet if they are asked subsequently which food the creature selected, or by what means it clung on to the apparatus, they often find they must look again and with more detailed, particular attention.

Here are some drawings made by seven-year-old boys, as a result of careful observation of pets that they were looking after. It will be noted that in recording observations, labelled drawings have much to commend them.

Mice teeth

My teeth

Rats teeth

A cat's teeth

These teeth are very sharp

Seven-year-old boys' labelled drawings.

Recorded observations frequently extend over a period of time. This is typical of weather records, for example. Here are notes kept by some six-year-old children on the growth of some plants:

28 April: Yesterday we planted mustard and cress on a big dish. The mustard seeds are yellow and the cress seeds are brown, the mustard seeds are bigger than the cress.

29 April: Our mustard and cress was planted on the 27th April and little roots are coming up on the seeds now. The cress seeds are brown and the mustard seeds are yellow.

30 April: There are little shoots coming up on our mustard and cress seeds and soon it will grow up into lovely juicy mustard and cress. The brown seeds are coming up and so is the yellow.

6 May: The mustard and cress is growing very tall now and the cress is green now.

7 May: Our mustard and cress is growing a lot and all the shoots are coming up and soon it will be grown. The cress is taller than the mustard.

8 May: Our cress seeds are 1 inch long and the mustard is a $\frac{1}{2}$ an inch long.

14 May: Our mustard and cress is growing a lot and Miss H. said it will soon be ready to cut. Cress $1\frac{1}{2}$ inches mustard $\frac{1}{2}$ an inch. The cress is growing the most but they are both growing a lot and soon we will be able to eat it.

From this very simple account it can be seen that the children's observations serve to develop their conceptual awareness of growth and, in particular, the relative growth rates between the two plants. It is worth repeating that good observation stems from interest, training, practice and evaluation. A pleasing example of this is seen in the following six-year-old's work:

> *Things noticed about Bimbo* (guinea pig).
> Bimbo was scratching himself with his back foot.
> Bimbo was washing himself with his front paws.
> Bimbo has 3 toes on his back feet and 4 on his front feet.
> Bimbo turned his head right round and washed the middle of his back.
> Bimbo eats oats and bran in the morning.
> I saw Bimbo washing underneath himself.

Such an activity would be made use of by a thoughtful teacher, leading on to consideration of wider issues such as, for example, grooming.

The teacher's role in preparing for detailed observation is illustrated in the following account of a trip to an airport by a group of six-year-old children.

> The children were all very excited this morning at the prospect of the visit to the airport tomorrow. I feel the discussion we had helped to calm the children a little, as they became interested in the various things we would be seeing on the visit.
> As many of the children's parents work at the airport, I found that they have a very good general idea of the sorts of things we are likely to find. We talked about the control tower, fire station, passenger buildings, fuelling depots, hangars, police station, etc. and their uses. This brought in some very useful words, and the discussion was lively and interesting.
> After the discussion . . . most of the children were so interested in the airport visit that they chose to write about this. The work that was done we stuck in the book made on the visit. In their writing I noticed a good deal of assimilation of

new words, e.g. at the beginning of the discussion only R. had
known what a hangar was, but now L. wrote 'We are going to
see the hangars.'

I feel the children have now some idea of what they can look
out for, which will mean they will probably observe a lot more
than they would have done otherwise.

There is a view that scientific method consists principally of a
bi-polar relation: on the one hand an imaginative component,
which contributes to the formation of hypotheses and theories
and, on the other, a critical component concerned with testing
theories. This is a view associated with such scientists as Whe-
well, Popper, Toulmin and N. R. Campbell. It is summed
up very concisely by Medawar [32] and also by Popper [45 p.
222]. Human knowledge began with the attempt to solve practical problems, and these strategies are the beginnings of the growth
of scientific knowledge. Faced with practical problems we set
up expectations, hypotheses or theories. We then proceed to
make selective observations and test our theory in order to
improve or modify it. Invariably we are left with a further
problem, for no solution is absolute. Such further problems we
may take up or leave, according to the needs of the moment.
Thus this sequence could be expressed as follows:

$$\text{problem}_1 \longrightarrow \begin{array}{c} \text{expectation} \\ \text{or tentative} \\ \text{solution} \end{array} \longrightarrow \begin{array}{c} \text{selective} \\ \text{observations} \\ \text{and tests} \end{array} \longrightarrow \text{problem}_2$$

Frequently the bringing together of two hitherto unrelated
pieces of learning leads to the solution of a new problem. This
constitutes a genuinely creative act of thought.

As the developing child builds up experience, so he has more
to bring to the solution of problems. The ability to bring past
learning to bear upon new problems depends upon making
assumptions about similarities in the world. This propensity
to look out for regularities is built into the human organism:
no mental development is possible where all phenomena are
interpreted as unique and discrete.

Each new event must in some measure be dealt with in
terms of past events. That such a basic need to find regularity
exists is confirmed by the satisfaction of children who achieve

such discoveries. A regularity that children are continually discovering is that one thing invariably leads to another, and so the notion of causality is born.

In a good infants' school the children will find answers to their questions but if we wish to lay the foundations of the scientific attitude we must build in an inter-subjective check by encouraging discussion and by the sharing of experience among children and teachers. The teacher's crucial role is to put further questions and to draw attention to factors hitherto overlooked, but yet within the comprehension of the children. This is frequently a matter of delicate judgment. In this way opportunities are made to set up experiments. From a teacher's notes:

> I talked to M., J. and N. at the water trough. Would the stone float or sink? Or the wooden blocks? Or the plastic bowls? etc. They were estimating correctly until they came to things with holes in them.
>
> A wooden cylinder with holes in it would sink, they thought: in fact it floated. A plastic cylinder would sink. It did. Why? One replied, 'Because it's got a hole in it.' 'But this one has a hole in it, and it floats.' 'This one is heavier,' said M., pointing to the plastic one. Are you sure? They weighed it, and found it lighter.
>
> ... And so the discussion continued; the children trying to solve the problem of what properties 'make' things sink or float.

This example was from some six-year-old children. Here is a more elaborate activity from some seven- and eight-year-old boys:

> During the Spring term several boys brought in toy cars.
>
> Initially the children were concerned with collecting, and cars were compared by type and make. At that time a television programme on weathering was shown, and there followed a general interest in discovering signs of weathering in the school garden. The slopes and gulleys in the wooded part of the garden were suddenly seen by two boys, not only as signs of weathering, but also as circuits on which to test their cars. Tests were made on speed and stability. They discovered that shape, weight, size, suspension and tyres all had various effects. The perfor-

mance of each car was noted. They fell into two main categories: those that went fast, but overturned or went off course; and those which were slower but more stable.

The children's findings were gathered and assessed in class discussions.

In the Summer term, some boys brought in two clockwork tanks, which they experimented with on a ramp, varying the degree of slope.

Meanwhile the 'car' group of boys decided to test their cars on this ramp. It was a long board of polished wood, and many of the small cars slipped on it. Sandpaper was bought from the classroom shop, and a renewed interest in tyre tread arose.

On the interest table the teacher then put articles worn away by friction, accompanied by a simple library book on it. The children began to bring things to add to the collection. Experiments were carried out with some of these materials, and the results were noted in two categories:

(i) those materials which get worn away;
(ii) those materials which wear away other things.

Topics and questions which arose in discussion were:

Heat produced by friction.

Jet aeroplanes need air cooling inside for passengers, because air outside heats the plane when it travels at high speeds.

Oil is needed for lubricating heated parts of car engines.

Does everything get hot if you rub it hard?

Do some things get worn away more quickly than others?

The scientist manifests an inquiring mind. He is not produced overnight, as it were, in the university; but his inquiring nature has been perpetuated and enriched from his earliest childhood. In short, it is suggested that there is a continuity here.

Our responsibilities as teachers do not extend just to potential scientists, for we do not know where the interests and enthusiasms that we foster in children will lead them. In fact, all of us need to have a rational view of the world, if we are to make sense of it. The attempt begins in the earliest explorations of childhood: the interest and curiosity are there initially. Our task is to see that they do not atrophy, because it is through them that we can acquire a truly scientific attitude of mind.

CHAPTER 3

Art: Representation and Expression

'Every art image is a purified and simplified aspect of the outer world, composed by the laws of the inner world to express its nature.' Susanne Langer [28].

In considering how to foster the artistic development of young children we are faced at the outset with two fundamental issues. Firstly, we need to understand how at this stage art relates to intellectual and emotional aspects of development. This is essential if we are to provide the conditions in which aesthetic development and these related aspects of intellectual and emotional growth can flourish. Secondly, we need to recognize both the continuities and the discontinuities between child art and adult art. Only then can we observe, evaluate and appreciate on the basis of a child's achievement and purposes, and avoid the pitfall of judging children's work by adult standards.

If we are to achieve this two-fold understanding it is crucial that we understand the 'laws of the inner world' to which Susanne Langer refers. This is no simple task, for some of these 'laws' are invariant and as true of children as they are of adults, but others are true of a certain stage in development. These can either be different from those of an earlier stage, or they can show certain modifications of earlier developmental characteristics. For example, imaging is a psychological process which is an important ingredient in the artistic expression of both children and adults; this is one of the continuities between child and adult art. There also occur differences, which will be outlined later, in the precise relationship of imagery to thought: these constitute one of the discontinuities between child and adult art, and a knowledge of them is

34

vital to an understanding of the artistic expression of young children.

In the previous chapter an account is given of the gradual construction of the idea that objects have a separate and permanent existence. When an infant has learned that something which has been put out of the immediate field of the senses, has a continued and separate existence, then he is able to form images. This is an acquisition which leads him to a new level of intellectual functioning. The idea that objects have a permanent existence is constructed during these first eighteen months to two years of life through sensory-motor activity. A child's activity is on objects that are present and visible, tangible or audible. In fact this sensory-motor activity is all that is available to an infant at this stage, for unless objects are understood to have a permanent existence there is no imagery through which a child can evoke the past and anticipate the future in the absence of present objects. Thought as distinct from sensory-motor activity must be concerned with what is absent, with what is past, and with anticipation. Children must be able to evoke what is absent or past in order to think about these, and this evocation requires a symbol to stand for what is not here and now. Representation is the means by which human beings organize their experience of the world in order to further their understanding of it. Representation requires symbols. Imagery is one way of symbolizing the world and language is another.

As soon as a child can represent [1] through imagery we see the beginning of behaviour which essentially involves the expression of imagery. On the one hand, there emerges symbolic play, and on the other hand (somewhat later), children begin to draw, to paint and to construct with various materials. Piaget's [42] study of the development of children's play shows that in their symbolic play they move through stages leading towards increasing realism. In the earliest stages of symbolic play a child is quite unconcerned that the expressive symbol he uses bears little resemblance to the internal symbol which he

---

[1] The term 'representation' is frequently used to denote both the internal symbol, the image, and the externalization of this internal symbol in drawing, painting, drama and so on. In order to avoid confusion 'representation' will be used here only to refer to the internal symbol, and the term 'expression' will be used to refer to the externalization of imagery.

is trying to express. For example, a two-year-old child, who pretends to drive a car and sits with his feet tucked under him, may be unconcerned if an adult points out that cars have various pedals. The roaring noises he makes and some vigorous but erratic movements with an imaginary steering wheel are sufficiently analogous at this stage. What is important is what is symbolized rather than the realism of the expressive symbol used, which is only in the nature of an analogy. This is true whether a child uses his own body as the expressive symbol, as in the above example, or uses an object as an analogy. For example, another two-year-old child fed her doll with a stick which symbolized a feeding bottle, then pretended to comb the doll's hair with the stick and finally, having put the doll to bed, she pretended to cook a meal using the stick as a spoon. The stick can quickly change from a feeding bottle to a comb and then again to a spoon because of its merely analogical character. Children are not concerned with realism at this stage.

The development of symbolic play shows a move towards increasing realism, towards a greater match between the symbolized and the expressive symbol, and through the first school years there is a gradual decline in analogical symbolization in favour of realistic symbolization.[1] While three-year-olds in the nursery school will use wooden blocks to symbolize tea cups for their tea party, children in the first school are concerned that the cups in their home play should be real cups, that the knobs on their model television set should turn, that their telephone has a movable dial and so on. By the time children have reached the top of the first school we can begin to speak of drama rather than symbolic play, for by now children begin to be concerned with precise detail in their dramatic play in order to achieve realistic effects. For example, some eight-year-old children, during the battle of Hastings celebrations, decided to act the story of the Norman conquest. They went to great lengths in consulting books and in acquiring suitable materials to make weapons and clothes which resembled what was historically correct.

The development from the gross analogy of a two-year-old to

---

[1] Paiget [42] defines play as the primacy of assimilation over accommodation. This means that the child is more concerned to fit the world to his ideas, his images (assimilation), than he is to change his ideas to fit the world (accommodation).

the realism of an eight-year-old is one of gradual transitions, in which there are both analogical elements and elements of imitation in which a child is more concerned to match reality. For example, some six-year-old children were enacting what they considered to be a hospital scene; they made up the bed with carefully considered precision after discussing the fact that the top sheet went under and not over the blankets. However, they were content to use a pencil as a makeshift thermometer and, even though there were bottles in the classroom, the child playing the part of the doctor handed over the nearest object to hand, a cardboard cylinder, as a bottle of medicine.

The expression of representations through drawing, painting, modelling and constructing go through stages similar to those outlined in symbolic play. At first there is nothing that can properly be called symbolic expression but rather a sensory-motor exploration of materials. The first pencilled scribbles of a two-year-old, a three-year-old's experiments with daubs or stripes of paint, the first conglomerations of boxes and tubes stuck together by a five-year-old experimenting with junk materials for the first time are all of this order. They are pre-symbolic. Questioned about what they are painting or constructing, at this stage children often reply that they do not know, or perhaps give their work a label only to please the adult. Plate 2 is an example of this sensory-motor exploration with materials. When he had finished it the child noticed the resemblance to a rocket and then named it. In the course of these early sensory-motor explorations with materials children learn to repeat certain lines and shapes, paying increasing attention to colours, textures and patterns. They then move into the next stage where the materials themselves or the first daubs of paint suggest the analogy and determine the content of their expressions; the bottle tops suggest wheels and the collage becomes a motor car: a piece of wood suggests the hull of a boat, and what began as an experiment with colour is seen as the outline of a house and determines the rest of the painting.[1]

[1] Of course, many adult artists find the initial inspiration for a work in some interesting piece of material or a shape produced at first in a random way. At this stage in children's development, however, the initial suggesting effect of the materials is only an aspect of their lack of concern with realism which does not stem from any attempt to produce an 'abstract', but is a reflection of a stage of intellectual development.

Questioned by an adult on the content of his work, a child at this stage will sometimes answer, 'I don't know because I have not finished it yet.' At this stage, as in the early stages of children's symbolic play, their expressions in paintings, drawings and constructions are largely analogical. A child is not concerned that his junk material boat has no prow, or that the wheels of the motor car he has made do not turn.

At the next stage a child decides on what he wishes to express first and selects his materials accordingly, but at first his expressions still have a largely analogical character. Plate 3 is an example of this analogical expression. Without the title it would be difficult to know what the painting expresses. From his answers to his teacher's questioning as he painted, it was evident that this child was concerned to express the circular motion of the bicycle wheels. From five to eight years children's expressions show a decline in the analogical and a move towards greater realism. As part of this realism first school children show increasing concern for precision and detail. Their constructions of boats acquire prows and portholes, and they become anxious that the wheels of the cars they make will turn. A seven-year-old boy, who had made a drum using a tin can and some rubber from the inner tube of a tyre, asked his teacher to teach him to sew so that he could make an outer fabric casing for his drum like the one that the teacher had put on the music table. Another seven-year-old made a junk material lorry, which tipped slightly backwards because the different materials he had used for the front and the rear of the vehicle created imbalance. He went to great lengths to collect a number of stones of different sizes, and he explored the weight they added to the front when stuck to the underside until he had achieved a balance. A six-year-old modelled a clay giraffe which would not stand up because the body was too heavy for the legs. He solved his problem by removing the clay legs and replacing them with matchsticks. This solution would have detracted from the realism desired by an eight-year-old who, faced with the identical problem, spent a great deal of time and patience cutting and straightening four equal lengths of wire to insert through the legs and into the body of the giraffe to reinforce them.

This increasing realism is illustrated in Plates 4 to 10. The faces of the rabbit and the elephant have a human look compared with the more realistic looking owl. Increasing detail is another aspect of the growth in realism. The trappings of St. George and his horse, and the feathers, beak, feet and large eyes of the owl show more attention to detail than the painting of the rabbit or the picture of the deer, where both the deers' antlers and the branches of the tree are expressed schematically as crosses.

All the stages described and the transitions between them appear in the first school years. The stage a child has reached is a matter of development, and this development is partly related to experience. There are two sorts of experiences which affect the development of children's expressions. The first is experience with materials. Three-year-old children in a nursery school frequently build a tower-like structure of bricks only to knock it down immediately. They are not so much concerned with the representation of a tower, as with exploring the balancing and collapsing qualities of brick structures. The very same activity can be seen among five-year-old children if they are using bricks for the first time. In the same way children introduced to clay for the first time, whether they are five or eight years old, explore its qualities in various ways, pummelling it, pulling it, squeezing it and bouncing it. They investigate the properties of the material in the same sensory-motor way as can be seen with much younger children in the nursery school. In the introductory chapter it is stated that 'if anything is certain about the learning process it is that one cannot miss out stages and hope to get a satisfactory end result', and this is as true of children's expressive work as of other areas of learning, though older children introduced to a new material for the first time will pass through this pre-symbolic stage of exploring the properties of materials more quickly than younger children.

Since children need to explore materials before they can go on to express their representations through them the provision of a variety of materials for creative expression is essential in the first school. Materials for modelling should include clay and wet sand. Clay is preferable to plasticine as it is more malleable. Bricks, junk material and wood should be available for constructional work, covering a range of shapes, sizes and textures. Adequate tools, glues and so on should also be provided. Materials for drawing and painting should include a range of colours and sizes of paper and a variety of brushes and other implements such as felt-tipped pens, thick and thin wax crayons and pencils. Collage materials too should cover a range of textures, colours and patterns.

Children need experience with materials to acquire skill in using various media, but there are other sorts of experiences which are crucial, for they are the experiences which give content to children's expressions. Understanding the relationship between experience and expressive work involves an understanding of the psychological nature of representation.

There is a popular notion of an image as a sort of photographic replica of a sense impression. It is a notion that implies a psychological passivity, in which exposure to sense impressions is all that is necessary for these replications in the form of images to be, as it were, printed. Bartlett's [4] experimental work on imagery shows that images are not replications but reconstructions, which may involve additions, omissions and distortions. In our experiences we are idiosyncratic; we each pay attention to different aspects of what from a purely external point of view seems to be the same 'experience' and the aspects we select to pay attention to and those we neglect depend largely on our previous experiences, on what we already know and understand. A teacher of a class of five-year-old children introduced some tame mice. Several children drew and painted the mice, and it was evident from their work that different children paid attention to different aspects of the animals, some to the whiskers, some to the tails, some to the feet and some to the ears. In fact we cannot strictly have the same experiences as others, for experiences are basically a personal matter. This is why images are essentially symbolic representations. They are not replications, but symbols of experiences through which we have lived and learned.

To foster children's representations, which in turn determine the content of their expressions, we need to provide the conditions that lead to the rich imagery which results not only from the quantity of experiences, but also from their quality. Reg Butler [10] says of an art student that his opportunities to create 'will be proportional to the variety, the richness, and the general intensity of the experiences to which he is exposed . . . but not only should the spectrum of experience be wide; the sequence of experience is also of very great importance'.

What is true of art students is true of children; they need not only a wide spectrum of experiences, but also a sequence of experiences, which relate to each other and which lead to increasing depth of understanding. Children can be given a number of experiences which are fragmented and lacking in depth. Visits to the park this week, the zoo next and the river the next, would be less desirable if they were to result in superficiality than one visit to the park, which is followed by inspection under the microscope of the specimens brought back, by discussion of their functions and attributes, by poems and stories read about them, by the collection of other related specimens and so on. There should be a quality of cumulativeness about the experiences we make available to children, which leads to depth in understanding as well as to variety of imagery.

One of the results of an inadequate experiential background is that children tend to perseverate at an earlier stage of development. They go on producing patterns or daubs which are largely in the nature of sensory-motor explorations, when they should be moving on to symbolic expression. Or their symbolic expressions are thin and they repeat the same stereotyped boats or houses which are primarily analogous, when they should be moving towards greater realism.

Reg Butler [10] has advised art students, 'Above all do not allow yourselves to visualize your final result, for to do so will inhibit your powers of discovery.' The implication here is that a greater measure of organization, understanding and control is made possible through expression. From five to eight years, when children are seeking more detail and precision in their increasing desire for realism, the opportunity to inspect the adequacy and appropriateness of their representations and thus to develop more organization, understanding and control is made possible through their expressive work, and is of great importance not just for their artistic development but for their intellectual development generally. Young children cannot examine their internal representations directly. This would involve the ability to turn round on one's own psychological processes, as it were, an ability which develops through the middle school years and appears only sporadically before eight years. It is through the externalization of their representations in various expressions that children can examine them to see how appropriate or adequate they are. We often see in the first school years how this examination of their expressions enables children to elaborate or modify their representations in mid-stream. One autumn, a teacher of a class of six-year-old children took them for a walk in the park. One of the things they looked at and discussed was the changing colour of the leaves. The next day one child drew in crayons a tree which possessed both a circular mass of green foliage and a number of highly coloured daubs around the circumference, which, she explained, were the autumn leaves. When the picture was almost completed this child realized its inappropriateness, turned over the sheet of paper, and drew another tree without the green foliage.

It was stated above that pictures by young children which are the result of sensory-motor experimentation with materials should not be confused with the abstract work of adult artists, for although there may be superficial resemblances between them there are underlying psychological discontinuities. Similarly an adult artist might decide to paint a tree with both green and autumnal foliage in order to express symbolically at one and the same time the characteristics of two seasons. But, again, this should not be confused with the unmodified picture in the above example, which was the result of a new discovery about trees superimposed on an established schematic expression. It is not only lack of experience but also lack of opportunity for expressing such experience which can lead to unsatisfactory development. Teachers who take over a class of children who have been deprived of opportunities for expression find that, when given these opportunities, what is produced at first resembles the work of much younger children. This is not entirely a matter of skill. Although they are clumsier with a brush or a pencil than their contemporaries who have had ample opportunities for expression, the content and form of their work is startlingly like that of younger children. A class of seven-year-old children from homes which had provided a rich experiential background had been deprived of opportunities for expression in school. When they were first given paper and paint their pictures were like those of five-year-olds; for example, many of them painted human figures in outline only, with few facial details, without necks, often with no hands and with hair around only the circumference of the head—all characteristics of the work of average five-year-old children. It was the control and organization of their representations which expression helps to develop that had been lacking.

The increasing realism illustrated by the children's paintings in plates 4 to 10 is not only a matter of greater detail. In plate 7 for example, relative sizes are ignored so that the cat, dog and horse are the same size, the girl is taller than the house, and the apple hanging from the tree is as large as the girl's head. At a later stage of development relative sizes are taken into account. In the pictures of the deer, and of the cat, dog and horse the sky is drawn as a strip at the top of the paper, while in plate 10, 'Horses', the horizon is successfully painted. In plate 5 the bars of the cage do not overlap the elephant, making it appear to be outside the cage rather than inside it as intended. In the eight-year-old boy's painting of horses (plate 10) successful overlapping gives the appearance of perspective.

These differences in perspective and proportion are not to be accounted for entirely by the move away from analogical expression already discussed. These other differences are a result of the growth of ideas of spatial relationships which has been elaborated by Piaget [44].

The imagery of the younger children in the first school appears to be of a partial and fragmented nature. The guardsman without body or arms in plate 1 illustrates the partial nature of imagery at this stage. This picture was painted after a visit to see the guards, and it is clear that this child was particularly impressed by the busby that the guardsman wore. In the drawing of the cat, dog and horse (plate 7) the elements are discrete and imagery appears fragmented because proportion is ignored.

Through the first school years children's paintings and drawings show increasing co-ordination of imagery. These changing characteristics are related to a child's conceptual development. Representation has already been defined as requiring symbolization, either in the form of imagery or language, but in the intellectual development of a child, from the moment that representation is first possible at between eighteen months and two years of age, on through the preschool and first school years, images gradually become embedded in a conceptual framework. Representation thus gradually becomes not simply a question of imagery but rather of images which inhere within certain relationships, including spatial relationships, which are increasingly understood and reproduced in a child's expressions.

Three stages of development which reflect the growth in understanding of spatial relationships can be seen in children's pictorial space. Adopting terms originally used by Luquet, Piaget calls these three stages (1) synthetic incapacity, (2) intellectual realism and (3) visual realism.

The first stage of synthetic incapacity is found in the preschool years and among younger children in the first school. It is at this stage that imagery appears partial and fragmented, because spatial relationships of proportion, distance orientation and perspective are neglected, and this neglect results in a failure to synthesize imagal elements. Plate 11, in which the car, road and pavement are quite discrete, illustrates an extreme example of synthetic incapacity.

The next stage in the development of pictorial space is termed intellectual realism, because the child does not draw or paint what he can actually see, but rather what he knows to be there. For example, a side view of a motor car may be drawn with all four wheels shown in succession, or a human figure may be drawn in profile but with both eyes and both arms included. The picture of the elephant (plate 5) is an example of intellectual realism: all four of the animal's legs are painted in succession, and both eyes, both ears as well as the nose and mouth are included, although the position of the trunk indicates a face in profile. In the six-year-old boy's painting (plate 13) of a horse and riders, both legs of the riders are shown on one side of the horse. This is characteristic of intellectual realism. Plate 12 is an example of transparency, another typical feature of this stage of development.

The third stage of visual realism appears on the average at nine to ten years of age, but can be seen in the work of some children towards the upper end of the first school. Visual realism does not mean that a child literally ceases to paint what he knows and now paints instead what he sees. Picasso has said, 'I paint not what I see but what I know', and there is a sense in which a child at the stage of visual realism also paints 'what he knows'. Some of the differences between intellectual realism and visual realism can be accounted for by the fact that at the stage of visual realism a child now knows more; what he now knows or understands are the relationships of objects to their spatial co-ordinates.

Plates 10 and 16 show the perspective effect which is achieved at this stage of visual realism. Plate 16 is a drawing by a six-year-old boy. It is the type of drawing which is much more characteristic of children of nine years or over, but this child was very advanced in this respect. A comparison of his drawing with plate 11 illustrates the range of individual differences that can be found in an infants' school.

There is no sudden move from one of these stages of development to another, but a smooth transition. Plates 14 and 15 illustrate this transition. In plate 14 the relative sizes of the boat, bridge and figures are inadequately expressed, but some sense of perspective is achieved with the clock tower building on the far bank. In plate 15 the front of the engine shows the beginning of an attempt to paint in perspective.

It has sometimes been suggested that the stage of visual realism represents a regression. The simple paintings and drawings of children at the stage of synthetic incapacity appear to be more naturalistic than those of children at the stage of intellectual realism with the strange transparencies, expansions and distortions that characterize it, while the overlapping and perspective which appear in the work of children at the stage of visual realism again make for more naturalistic-looking work than that of the preceding stage. It is this apparent return to a more naturalistic type of expression at the stage of visual realism which has led to the suggestion that children at this stage have regressed to a more primitive type of expression. But to interpret these characteristics of visual realism as a regression is to apply inappropriate criteria concerning naturalistic art instead of appropriate criteria concerning children's psychological development.

As Herbert Read [46] has shown, some attempts to categorize

children's art have also been impaled on the horns of the dilemma of the place of the percept and the concept in children's expressions. It has sometimes been suggested that at the stage of intellectual realism children paint 'what they know', while at the stage of visual realism they paint 'what they see', in other words, that in the former stage concepts, and in the latter stage percepts, are expressed. This would be paradoxical and would constitute a true regression, for developmentally percept precedes concept. It has been shown in Chapter 6, for example, that at the stage which Piaget calls 'intuitive', approximately between the ages of five and seven, children respond to tests involving certain mathematical relationships in ways which seem illogical to adult minds. They believe, for example, that certain substances change in quantity if they are transformed in various ways, and that certain quantities are increased or decreased if their configurations are changed. For example, a ball of clay becomes more or less if it is rolled into a sausage, a quantity of liquid becomes more or less if it is poured into a container of a different size, and a number of objects become more if they are spread out and less if they are pushed closer together. Children at the intuitive stage make these judgments on the basis of certain perceptual aspects of the situation, such as the length of the clay or the height of the vessel containing the liquid, and they have not yet acquired the concepts of conservation necessary to an understanding of the mathematical relationships involved. Similarly in children's expressive work it is the stage of visual realism which is conceptual and the preceding stages which are perceptual, not the reverse. Children's work at the stage of visual realism seems more naturalistic, more like 'what they see', precisely because their spatial concepts have developed to the point where they can reconstruct objects in relation to two-dimensional and three-dimensional co-ordinates, and can therefore produce pictures which have perspective.

Other concepts as well as spatial concepts affect the form of children's paintings. The child who painted Peter who had German measles (plate 17) clearly does not understand contagion, and believes that the symptomatic spots are directly caught.

Children at the stage of visual realism, of course, do base

their work on closer observation than previously. This is part of the move towards greater realism in their expression, which has already been described. It is important at this stage that teachers help children to avoid superficial copying. Children's observations should not stop short at the surface appearance of things, but should lead to greater understanding of relationships. For example, an eight-year-old girl showed interest in some fruit and vegetables which the teacher had taken into school, and decided to paint a still-life of them. Her first attempt was poor, and she herself was dissatisfied with it. It was copying on the basis of very superficial observation; a brussels sprout which had been sliced vertically in half was reproduced as a series of concentric circles crossed by an ill-defined line which was meant to be the stalk. Before the girl began her second attempt the teacher discussed with her the way the stalk tapered gradually from the base, the way the leaves grew from the stalk, and the differences in thickness of these from the base up. She thus deepened this child's observations, and helped her to relate what she saw to an understanding of the growth of the vegetable. In this way she took the child from a simple perceptual level to a more conceptual level of understanding. The picture which was the result of her second attempt was of a much higher standard.

The more naturalistic work which children begin to produce at the upper end of the first school is influenced in part by the forms of expression common in our culture, for cross-cultural differences in children's artistic work begin to emerge at this age. Children gradually assimilate a certain 'vocabulary' from the artistic models to which they are exposed. The provision of work of aesthetic value, in painting, in sculpture, in pottery is important. These provide models which are necessary to artistic development. The models teachers present should therefore cover a wide range of diversity of form and style, so that children assimilate alternative 'vocabularies', and can select at various times what is appropriate to their own purposes.

It was suggested at the beginning of this chapter that in order to understand children's artistic expressions we must know both the discontinuities and the continuities between child and adult art. The nature and stages of children's development have been elaborated in relation to their expression, and these illustrate some of the discontinuities. The second part of this two-fold task, that of understanding what continuity there is between the artistic expressions of children and adult artists is notoriously difficult, for it involves the vexed question of what art is. There is a confusion of aesthetic notions among artists, philosophers and teachers, a confusion which, as Langer points out, is not made less muddled by the fact that theories on the nature of art may start by asking one of two quite different questions. The first type of theory attempts to answer basic questions on the nature of the feelings and ideas that are aroused in an observer by a work of art. The second type of theory attempts to provide answers to questions about the nature of artistic activity. It is primarily concerned with the motivation of the artist and other psychological processes that are involved in creative activity. This latter category of theory would seem to be of more value in an examination of the continuities between children's expressions and adult art, for to examine children's work in terms of criteria which relate to the effect of a work of art on an observer could involve judging children's work by adult standards.

Susanne Langer, who has made one of the most comprehensive attempts to derive a theory of art in terms of the artist's psychological processes, calls a work of art an 'art symbol'. The word symbol in this context is used in a rather special sense. If one person says to another, 'I saw a sunset last night', he is using language to stand for a past event; the words refer to something that existed apart from the words, and they are instruments for communicating something in the absence of a shared, contemporaneous experience. The words are in this case discursive symbols, but a poem about a sunset is in a different category: it is a non-discursive symbol which expresses certain ideas about feelings in the context of a sunset, which cannot be grasped apart from the total poetic form which expresses it. Pictorial art also performs this non-discursive function. In the words of Langer [29] a work of art is a symbol in the special sense that it has 'the power of formulating experience, and presenting it objectively for contemplation, logical intuition, recognition, understanding. . . . It formulates the appearance of feeling, of subjective experience, the character of so-called "inner life", which discourse—the normal use of words—is peculiarly unable to articulate, and which, therefore, we can only refer to in a general and quite superficial way.'

Since the art symbol expresses ideas about feelings, it embodies subjective experience which is affective as well as cognitive. It has already been stated that the images which children express in art forms involve what is personally significant to them. This personal significance has an affective as well as a cognitive character and constitutes the continuity between child and adult art. The children who selected different aspects of the mice to pay attention to, and who emphasized these different aspects in their pictures, did not make this selection in a haphazard way. They were appraising different aspects of the mouse; their pictures denote not simply idiosyncratic imagery, but personal affective experience too. Of course young children's work cannot be expected to embody ideas about feelings at the same level of sophistication as an adult artist. Often the affective aspect in children's expressive work is simply at the level of a temporary interest, like that of a six-year-old girl who was particularly interested in the shutters and carport that were part of a house she visited for the first time which she subsequently depicted with great care. But a stronger emotional element is present in some of the creative work of young children, and this cannot be doubted if children are observed at their work. On a week-end trip to the country a seven-year-old girl saw a mare give birth to a foal. She arrived at school on Monday morning obsessed with the desire to paint this, and the care with which she experimented with different mixes of consistency and colour in order to produce the moist, warm and slightly foaming appearance of the newly born foal clearly indicated a powerful affective experience.

Clearly, if we are to foster children's artistic development, they must have opportunities both to evaluate and to express those experiences which have for them an affective significance. That there should be a quality of cumulativeness about the experiences we make available to children, which leads to representational elaboration, has already been stated. This cumulative quality also helps children to savour the quality of an experience in order to express its affective aspects.

It is through the provision and supplementing of experience with poems read, stories told and so on, that a teacher can foster artistic development, not through giving children topics to direct the content, nor through instructing children in technical tricks. Teachers who complain that their children have no imagination are describing not a 'disease' but a 'symptom', and the 'symptom' may be caused by paucity of experience, by inadequate materials or because the children have been deprived of previous opportunities for creative work.

When an art symbol is described as the embodiment of personally significant ideas or feelings, one cannot separate the ideas from the material through which they are expressed. If a diversity of materials is available to children, then each has an opportunity to select what is appropriate to the expression of his particular experience. Scrap materials consisting only of boxes will not give rise to very imaginative products because the selection is too restricted. A child who was entranced with the subtleties of colour of an autumn sunset could not express this adequately if he were given only four primary colours and not allowed to mix them; the affective aspect of his experience would not be carried over into an evaluative art symbol under these conditions.

The development of high standards is an important part of art education. If children have something to express which they feel is worth expressing, time in which to express it and the materials with which to do so adequately, then the conditions have been provided for the development of standards. This growth of skill in the use of tools and media is an inseparable part of selecting materials and executing the work with care in order to express what is personally significant, with adequate materials and tools to do so. If we understand this we shall not fall into the trap of by-passing this long process by giving children short-cuts to produce false standards. If children are shown how to cut round templates or how to stick cotton wool on to the outlines of lambs drawn by the teacher in order to make an Easter frieze, the result may be pleasing to the teacher and the children may have received some training in manual dexterity, but this sort of activity in no way contributes to children's artistic development.

A work of art has a function in extending human experience.

Since its form expresses certain ideas about feelings which cannot be fully grasped separately from this form, it can give new insights to the observer. It can deepen understanding or enlarge it with new facts and new interpretations and can refine feelings. This function has significance for both the development of children's creative potentiality and for their aesthetic development which may be even more important. Not all children can become adult artists, but our concern in education should be for the development of aesthetic appreciation in all children. It has already been suggested that exposure to works of aesthetic value, to paintings, to sculpture, to pottery, can provide models for an artistic 'vocabulary'. At the same time they should contribute to a deeper understanding, a refinement of affective life and to the development of aesthetic sensibility.

CHAPTER 4

Literature: Impression and Reflection

IT WOULD be true to say of many, if not most, teachers that their first encounter with a group of children involved the telling of a story. This is because the opportunity to listen to a story produces an immediate response from children and is one of the surest ways of establishing a rapport between them and an adult. It is not easy to know how this happens. While the power of great literature to gain and hold attention can be appreciated, with children the same result can be achieved with a comparatively trivial story, and many teachers have been puzzled by the rapt attention given by a whole class of young children to one of their number telling a long and sometimes incoherent story. It is clear that story-telling can evoke an intellectual and emotional response from children which is deeply satisfying. Adults gain this communal satisfaction at the theatre or cinema, and for children the physical presence of the teller is important. This is recognized in such wireless programmes as 'Listen With Mother': when these programmes are used in school, the teacher's presence still seems to be necessary as a representative of the unseen story-teller.

Part of the emotional satisfaction may arise from the personal relationship which is set up between the individual listeners and the story-teller. Although the story is told to a group of perhaps forty children, each child hears his own personal story and pays attention to the features which are relevant to *him*. In this way, the semblance of an intimate and highly personal relationship between him and the teller is established.

This personal relevance in a child's response to a story draws attention to an important aspect of any art form. A person looking at a picture or listening to a story responds to this in so far as he recognizes in it something of his own feelings, behaviour or experience. It is this recognitory aspect which probably accounts for the powerful attraction of a story, for it results in assimilatory activity in the child, enabling him to repeat, confirm or clarify feelings and experiences which have been important to him. There is a sense in which stories and poetry are play situations in which feelings about, or responses to, experiences outside the present and immediate can be assimilated.

However literature also gives rise to accommodatory behaviour, presenting a variety of alternative possible developments or solutions. These accommodations may lead to further insights into existing situations, for example reading Blake's 'The Little Black Boy' might have a contribution to make to children's thinking on current colour problems, or may go further and produce a change in an individual's behaviour. Reading George Eliot's treatment of the relationship between Adam Bede and his mother enabled a person to gain greater understanding of the behaviour and feelings of her elderly mother, and this led to a change in behaviour towards her.

Literature often brings about further accommodations to sensory experience. It is a common experience to find one's perception of some 'ordinary' object enhanced by a poet's description (cf. Art, p. 51): thrush's eggs appear a brighter blue when we look at them through the eyes of the poet:

> And by-and-by, like heath bells gilt with dew,
> There lay her shining eggs, as bright as flowers,
> Ink-spotted over shells of greeny blue.

And no one who has watched a bird building its nest could fail to deepen this experience when reading:

> I watched her secret toil from day to day—
> How true she warped the moss, to form a nest,
> And modelled it within with wood and clay.

> (John Clare)

Another function of any art form is that it brings some kind of order to the complexity of experiences which living produces.

This order may be concerned with ideas or emotions. Dickens's description of Maggie in *Little Dorrit* helps the reader to order his ideas of the effects of mental retardation, or again, his ideas of the conditions in nineteenth-century prisons.

By concentrating on a precise idea combined with a highly conscious and condensed use of language poetry may bring a very tight structure to experience. This is demonstrated, for example, in Shakespeare's examination of the concept of mercy in Portia's speech in *The Merchant of Venice* or in W. H. Davies's reflection on time in his poem 'Leisure'.

This applies equally to children's use of literature. As with adults, various factors will determine the recognitory response made to a story or poem and to what aspects attention is paid. A recent experience or dominant interest will influence choice and attention, while a present mood or more lasting emotional state may lead to great absorption. The difference in the response of children is in the comparative immaturity both of their emotions and of the level of intellectual structuring brought to bear on the situation.

For most babies the first response to literary experience is to action rhymes. The enjoyment of rhymes such as 'This little pig' and 'Round and round the garden' is in the pinching and tickling inseparable from them. Thus it is the sensory-motor actions which embody the recognitory function in these rhymes. The language is incidental, acting as a signal for the accompanying actions. Any rhymes can lead to sensory-motor recognition if actions are added to them. A one-year-old sitting on an adult's lap ignored 'Humpty Dumpty' until she was slipped between the adult's knees when Humpty fell off the wall. After this the preceding lines were enjoyed only in anticipation of this action.

The developing ability to symbolize in image and language leads to the enjoyment of stories and rhymes which represent experiences—the 'recognitions' referred to earlier. Three- and four-year-olds respond readily to onomatopoeic language and enjoy stories which include, for example, animal and everyday sounds—the 'clinking' of milk bottles, 'thumping' of feet or 'buzzing' of aeroplanes.

Children only slowly learn the meaning of words such as 'sad' and 'happy' as these are used to describe their own actions, for example, crying and laughing. So at first they will recognize feelings in story characters only in the description of such behaviour. Stories make an important contribution towards the slow learning of language to represent *feelings* by not only describing a variety of situations but also the emotional responses of the characters. In this way children are helped to recognize and put a name to feelings they have experienced. *Peter Rabbit* by Beatrix Potter is a good example of a story which is satisfying at this stage for it contains not only reference to emotional behaviour, e.g. 'sobbing', 'trembling', but also introduces language to describe feelings underlying such behaviour, e.g. 'frightened', 'excitement'. The characters of the story in which the feelings are manifest are largely incidental. It is not necessary to have any knowledge of rabbits to appreciate this story. It is about getting into, and out of, trouble and the accompanying feelings, and it is these aspects which are recognized by children. This is not to suggest that content is irrelevant. A satisfactory balance is necessary between idea and incident if the whole is to be understood by children, and the setting should not be totally unfamiliar to them. It is difficult to imagine what assimilatory or accommodatory activity was open to a class of children aged six years in East London, including a group of West Indians, who were told the story of an Eskimo boy living in an igloo.

Since very young children are still in the egocentric position of not being able to put themselves into the position of an imagined boy or girl they respond best to stories in which they are the main characters, or in which the plot or content resembles closely their own actions or experiences. This need for personal reference is still observable in nursery children and in young infants, when a story about a particular child or about a model which has been made will produce intense interest. As the shift away from egocentricity takes place children are able to put themselves into the position of imagined persons and situations (provided these bear adequate relation to themselves) and therefore begin to appreciate stories of increasing complexity. Stories, indeed, can make an important contribution to the decentering process by encouraging children to put themselves into the position of other persons, thereby elaborating their 'views' of people and experiences. Further, one story can give the differing impressions of a number of characters, thus encouraging a child to look at a situation from different points of view. *Big Sister and Little Sister* by Charlotte Zolotow, for example, looks at the relationship from the point of view of both sisters, an illustration of the structuring function literature can perform. This story can serve as an illustration of the play aspect of literature referred to earlier as it provides an abstraction of experience which 'plays' with ideas among others, of caring, loss, sadness and happiness.

The combination of these aspects of play and abstraction which a story incorporates encourages the move from play to thought. This is particularly important in relation to social and ethical understanding for while scientific knowledge can be tested and confirmed or negated by reference to concrete situations, it is not possible for all social and ethical knowledge to be tested in this way. Stories therefore can provide opportunities of reflecting on these situations both in setting out possibilities for consideration, and in allowing children to test out ideas in their own stories.

Children's response to stories and poetry keeps pace with their intellectual development as they move from pre-operational to operational levels of thought (cf. Chapter 9). The development of plot in 'The Gingerbread Man' or 'The House that Jack Built' does not demand conservation of thought in the listeners as the repetitive form continually reminds them of the sequence of the story. This helps to explain why repetitive stories are so popular with younger children while those older, who can hold a sequence of events in mind as a story develops, find them irritating and boring.

Children accommodating to the idea of seriation are fascinated by stories such as 'The Three Bears' and 'The Littlest Fir Tree' in both of which the notion of seriation is a key to appreciating the development of the plot. Or again, Wanda Gag's 'Millions of Cats' is particularly absorbing to those children who have just developed the notion of one-to-one correspondence.

'The Ugly Duckling' is appreciated and therefore enjoyed by children who have developed conservation and reversibility. The plot of this story requires a level of conceptual development involving stable temporal and spatial relationships and of the subtle differences between ducks and swans. Without this level of thought it is not possible to hold in mind the slow transformations of the Ugly Duckling and the effect of these on the other characters in the story.

Whilst the discussion so far has been concerned mainly with the match between stories and the intellectual understanding of children, reference has also been made to the relationship with emotional response. Intellectual and emotional response are recognized as interdependent. A child's emotional response is towards *what* or *whom* the story or poem is about, though how he is feeling at the moment will influence what he pays attention to in the story. As was suggested earlier, literature is in the unique position of being able to 'represent' any of life's countless experiences because verbal expression can be more precise, and explicit perhaps than any other art form. What is more, these 're-presentations' are likely to be in differently arranged relationships, and may therefore arouse either previously experienced or different emotions. In this way children's emotional response can be helped to develop in complexity and subtlety. Further, it is possible for a child to identify himself with any of the characters and therefore to experience something of the conflicting emotions which the same situation may arouse in each. The manner in which a story is told, and the emphases made by the teller will certainly affect the listener's response. In this way, an adult, through the medium of literature, can influence the development of emotions in children—and also of attitudes and values as is suggested in Chapter 8.[1]

It may be that during the first school period stories provide the opportunities for recognizing and clarifying emotions while creative materials provide for testing out and clarifying ideas. It is clearly evident from the powerful attraction of both that they satisfy fundamental needs in children of this age.

The appeal of stories for children sometimes leads to their use specifically for giving information. In the light of the discussion earlier in this chapter, this does not seem to be appro-

[1] In this context it is perhaps important to draw attention to unsatisfactory attitudes towards social issues, which children's literature may reinforce. For example, to what extent might the stupidity of Epaminondas feed into colour prejudice?

priate. It has been suggested that an author or poet interprets experiences imaginatively and, what is more, that the hearer then interprets these in terms of his understanding and level of maturity. It is a highly personal interpretation of what in the story is true *for him*, rather than what is objective or scientific truth. Information may be passed on, but this is incidental to the story and not its main function. To use stories for teaching scientific, historical or geographical facts is to invite children to interpret objective material in a subjective manner which may result in a confusion of fact and fiction. It is important here to note a difference in response between adults and young children to literature. An adult can distinguish between fiction and the various factual accounts of experience given for example in biography and travel. Children at this stage, with their limited experience and understanding, are not in a position to differentiate between the two. For them the story form is essentially imaginative, and their interpretation can slip into phantasy without the necessity or possibility of testing or confirming the conclusions drawn. Towards the end of the first school, however, the question 'Is it a true story?' which is asked by some children is an indication that literary categories of fiction and non-fiction are being developed.

Further, material in 'information' stories may be confusing or even inaccurate as, for example, nature stories in which animals are given human characteristics and include statements such as: 'Timmy Tadpole watched his tail getting smaller and wondered how he would be able to swim and play with his brothers and sisters.' It is not possible for a child to prove or disprove such a notion. An irrelevant inaccuracy has been introduced to him which he will have to disentangle later. As is discussed in Chapter 2, children need to learn scientific information from personal observation of animals, materials, etc. in the classroom, and in discussion with the teacher who can give further information. A teacher will also give facts or see that information books or pictures are available for children to gain further understanding of situations which cannot be personally observed; information, for example, about boats, aeroplanes or wild animals. It is probably true to say that information of this kind which has to be presented in story form in order to make it palatable for young children is in some way unsuitable.

Both stories and poetry make an important contribution towards children's language development by introducing new words in context. The writings of Beatrix Potter are a good illustration of this. In *The Flopsy Bunnies* the following words, not usually in the vocabularies of children of this age, are found:

> soporific, improvident, degrees, overcome, slumber, sufficiently, apologized.

Part of the fascination of her books lies in her use of words which catch children's attention by their sound and of which the meaning is within their experience.

By concentrating on the precise use of words to convey meaning, poetry maximizes the under- and over-tones of words and helps children to gain knowledge of the subtleties, complexities and beauty of the English language. A child's poem, 'The Saffron Butterfly' by Teresa Hooley illustrates this:

> Out of its dark cocoon,
> Like a blossom breaking earth
> A saffron butterfly
> Came to its April birth,
> Fluttered by banks of primroses.
> I could not tell, not I,
> If yellow butterflies starred the hedge,
> Or a flower flew in the sky.

The development of language during this stage leads not only to greater understanding and use of vocabulary but also to an interest in words themselves. Poetry heightens the awareness of words and also opens the possibility of creating new words. Rhymes and poetry such as 'Hickory, Dickory, Dock', 'Higglety, Pigglety my black hen' or 'Applecum Jockeby' in Walter de la Mare's 'Blindman's In' can often stimulate children to create new words for themselves.

The recognition and appreciation of rhythm found in longer rhymes and poems such as 'Simple Simon' and 'Mr. Nobody' would seem to be related to the recognition of the beat in music discussed in Chapter 7. Response to both appears to occur at about the same time towards the end of the first school. This real awareness of rhythm which is demonstrated as

children read or recite such poems is not to be confused with
the monotonous sing-song which can become attached to the
speaking of poetry by younger children.

Because poetry is for most children a much less familiar
literary form than stories, teachers of young children have the
special opportunity of introducing it to them probably for the
first time. In many instances it can focus attention on a specific
emotional or intellectual aspect of experience, for example,
Thomas Hardy's 'Weathers' or John Keats' 'Naughty Boy'
who

> ran away to Scotland,
> the people for to see.

In so doing it can help children to discover new depths in
everyday experience.

In this connection nursery rhymes provide a rich source of
poetic experience for young children. Iona and Peter Opie [36]
suggest that they have survived because of the 'one quality of
memorability' and are therefore poems which have satisfied
children over many centuries. It would be sad if this part of
our past were lost.

So far literature has been considered in its oral form, i.e.
as being read or told to children, but during the first school
period, of course, most children learn to read and their opportunity for literary experience is thus greatly extended. This is
not true for all children. At the end of this period some will
only just be beginning to make a formalized approach to
learning to read, while others will be fluent readers, finding
great satisfaction in books. It is not proposed, here, to consider
techniques in learning to read, but to draw attention to principles which should underlie children's reading, whatever
method of teaching is being used.

Reading is an extension of language development. Language
is grounded in and develops out of personal experience, enabling an individual to codify, clarify and extend his understanding of objects, situations and relationships. Reading
performs the same function, but provides much greater opportunities, by making available to one person the cumulative
thought of others.

It has been said that knowledge is universal but learning is personal, and this needs to be emphasized in relation to reading. A child must himself see the purpose in reading and find that his personal experience is illuminated or extended thereby. What he reads must have a meaning to him: the mere reading of 'words' lacks any purpose, as it can be a mechanical skill having no effect on his intellectual and emotional life.

In the first place, therefore, he must perceive that visual verbal signs are representations of oral verbal signs and thus of experience, and in the second place he must discover that these signs not only represent, but also extend experience. No one can teach a child these facts, but it is one of the most important functions of the first school to put children in the way of learning them. Learning to read can add a new dimension to the life of a child and the major responsibility for making it possible for this to take place rests on the teachers of young children. Most are fully aware of this responsibility, but this can lead to over-anxiety and pressure to achieve results. However, much anxiety is allayed when it is recognized that the most satisfactory learning situations exist in schools where books are an essential and integral part of the environment, where teachers naturally and frequently refer to books themselves and share them with the children, and where there is a basic expectation that most of the children will be able to read at seven years of age. In such schools only the children with particular intellectual or emotional difficulties fail to respond. It must be remembered that the adult's ability to read brings great pleasure and satisfaction to a child, and, as with other admired skills, is one which he will be anxious to achieve.

Children who come to school linguistically deprived have their own special problems, and for these one of the important functions of a school will be the development of oral language: written language may have to wait. However, the recognition of the problem is likely to lead to satisfactory attempts to solve it, especially if, in such instances, the junior schools accept the responsibility for introducing these children to reading.

Whatever degree of reading skill is achieved in the first school, the spoken story or poem is still important. Reading is essentially a private experience encouraging personal reflection, while the spoken word is a communal activity often producing a deeper emotional response. Both aspects are important. The shared experience of a story contributes both to the individual child and to the total life of a classroom. When visiting a theatre with friends most people are aware that personal appreciation and enjoyment is heightened when it is shared. This is true also of an individual child who can discover similar social satisfaction when listening to a story or poem, and as a result be helped in his social development. Such a shared experience can also provide a starting-point for discussion among children, which may develop interest in other areas of the classroom. For example, the story of 'The Little Red Engine' told to a class of five-year-olds led to a series of paintings, models, music and counting of coaches and engines in which the whole group was interested because of the original communal stimulus.

Opportunities must be provided for hearing and reading a wide variety of stories, poetry and books if we are to satisfy the literary needs of a whole class. This variety must allow for a wide range of content and complexity which will match the mental and emotional levels of the children. Book corners and libraries can be equipped with a changing supply which will sustain and develop individual and group interests. Many schools recognize the importance of making book corners attractive areas of the classroom where the provision of rugs, comfortable chairs and flowers adds to the enjoyment of the books.

Adequate material for oral story and poetry for a class of young children is more demanding of the teacher, since she must have a wide repertoire of suitable literature. If this is lacking the children may have very limited literary experience, and there is a temptation to present to young children simplified versions of classical literature more suitable for older children. The need to simplify such material indicates that it is unsuitable and is likely to deprive children of later appreciation of complexity of plot and vocabulary. Although some of 'The Just-So' stories, for instance, in their original form may be appropriate for children at the end of the first school, to simplify them for five-year-olds is to do a disservice both to children and to Rudyard Kipling. Older children will appreciate the complexity and excitement of myths and legends. The story of the

Wooden Horse of Troy or those about King Arthur provide a satisfying extension to their earlier enjoyment of traditional fairy stories.

The content of many traditional fairy stories is also inappropriate for young children. The concentration on fantasy, often of an aggressive kind, militates against the struggle for reality in which children of this age are involved. One cannot, however, be dogmatic about suitable literature. The choice will be dependent on many factors of interest, intellectual ability, etc. but it is important to ensure that children are given sufficient choice both for personal satisfaction and as an introduction to the wealth of our literature. Emphasis on certain types of story such as those about animals or fantasy to the exclusion of material based on children's everyday experiences may limit or deflect their appreciation.

In this connection also, the needs or problems of individual children must be borne in mind. The value of stories as a shared experience of a whole class has been discussed but some are unsuitable for particular children. For example, in one class a boy so quickly became over-stimulated that it was not possible to tell some exciting stories which the rest would have enjoyed. Again, one child or a small group can appreciate a story or poem which would be meaningless or boring to the rest. For this reason the allocation of 'story' to a set time of day for a whole class is too restricting, especially if this always comes at the end of the afternoon when the children are tired. Opportunities need to be taken during the day for small or larger groups to listen to a story or poem which is particularly appropriate for them. For example, some seven-year-olds feeling the effects of cold weather enjoyed 'When icicles hang by the wall', while the story of 'The Good Tractor' appealed to a younger group making a model of a tractor. It is at such times when interest and feeling are intense that the introduction of literary material is most likely to lead to further assimilatory and accommodatory activity and can become part of a child's total response.

Poems and stories repeated at the request of children because they are particularly enjoyed are learned, at least in part, and repeated. In a class of five-year-olds a boy watching the pet mouse recited, 'Three Blind Mice' quietly to himself, while a girl with a group of children round her told 'The Tale of the Turnip'.

Satisfaction from the retelling of stories and poems they have heard encourages children to create stories of their own. Many will have begun to do this before coming to school, telling 'stories' to adults, other children, animals or toys, but during first school the relationship is learned between oral and written language. The written expression of ideas is preceded by pictorial representation: pictures are drawn and the story told either as the picture develops or after it is completed. It is important to note this sequence of a story following a picture. Only later, when writing ability is more fully developed, is it usual for illustrations to follow the story, and often when this stage is reached an illustration is no longer considered necessary because the written expression is complete in itself.

Early writing demonstrates the limitations of pre-operational thought noted in other areas. Stories tend to be fragmented and however simple the plot this may lack continuity. Two examples of five-year-old work accompanying pictures illustrate this, one read

'A spotted dog, me, gold and a thunderstorm,'

another,

One day a little girl found a magic purse of gold in a forest. Then she went home and she had her tea and then she went out to play.

These are brief examples, but young children, though unable to write easily, can often dictate long stories to an adult. This creates problems for a teacher with a large class but it is important for this to be done whenever possible so that a child can relate his spoken story to its written form. A young child's writing ability is often so limited that to require him to write for himself is likely to result in a brief phrase not representing the quality of thinking that accompanied the original illustration. The following story was dictated by a boy just six years old, and accompanied a painting of three owls:

This is the story of three owls and the farmyard birds what was very naughty. They were getting very naughty except one who was not so bad, and the two owls were even better than the peacock. One of the birds who was a peacock went up to the owls and he said, 'Why do you live so happily?' So they explained how they lived so happily. 'This is how. We like watching these little creatures, like the little spiders but when it comes to be winter we fly away to somewhere new in a warmer country, and we stay there until the winter has gone and the flowers has opened and the spider webs are made and then we come back and go in a shady place.' But the farm birds just laughed and went back to their yard and started fighting. But the peacock stopped them and said, 'It is quite true that they live happily like that, and they told me before I asked them—that sometimes they go to the forest and the wood. That is the real truth what they said and I believe it—if you don't, I do.' The other two said very happily, 'We agree, it is the truth.' The peacocks said 'Good!' and went off to the owls and they said 'Good! Now winter's coming, and we shall have to be going in a week's time, and I hope you see us again, and when we come back we will bring a baby.'

The inconsistency of some of the detail in the story is typical of this stage, but the idea of happiness is sustained throughout in sensitive language. The child could not have written down such a story himself. He was in a 'vertically grouped' class, one of the advantages of which is that only a comparatively small group of children will require this kind of help at any one time.

Children of this age also begin to use poetry as a means of expressing ideas and feelings. The following poem was dictated by a five-year-old when it was very windy a few days after she had heard the story of 'The Old Woman who lived in a Vinegar Bottle':

> Wind, wind,
> Blowing north,
> Blowing south,
> Raining,
> Blowing,
> Hats are coming off.

As, during first school, children gain skill in writing and confidence in verbal expression, their stories and poetry reflect their intellectual and emotional development. This is demonstrated in the increasing complexity and sensitivity of ideas and feelings expressed and in the structure which they can bring to their reflection and organizing of experience. By the end of the first school, the writing of many children reflects the level of operational thought they have reached. Complicated plots can be developed and completed, and the stories are often long and sometimes written in chapters in book form. The following shorter story illustrates the structure and completeness typical of children at this stage:

The Very Wicked King

Once upon a time there was a very wicked King. Now this King was a very rich King and he loved money. At night he used to steal it from the people in the valley below. In the morning when the people got up and saw all the money had gone they were very cross. So they sent for all the wise men in the village and they had a meeting together. At last one of the men said, 'All of us shall surround the King's fort then when he comes out of his fort we can fight him and I hope we win.' All of the other people thought this a very good idea. That night when the King came out and started to go down the valley the other soldiers began to follow him. At last the soldiers caught up and surrounded the King. Then the soldiers said, 'Why did you steal our money and take our sheep?' Then the King said 'I will never do it again.' And they all lived happily ever after.

The arrival of a guinea-pig in their classroom was commemorated by three girls co-operating to write the following poem:

Our Guinea Pig

A guinea-pig
Has come to stay
With us.

The guinea-pig
Was frightened
Of us.

The guinea-pig's
Called Stripples
By us.

> The guinea-pig
> Looks black and brown and white
> To us.
>
> Our guinea-pig's
> Alright now
> With us

All the examples so far have been of imaginative writing, but children also use verbal expression to describe interesting personal experiences. A five-year-old wrote this about himself:

> I am going to school with my Mummy. My Daddy is seeing us off. We have to cross a road. Daddy says, 'Do your coat up.'

While a seven-year-old in a rural school wrote:

> Our sow pigged last night and she had eight piglets. And Daddy was up the whole night. And she is a quiet sow. She does not walk on the piglets. And we have three piglet pets, and they are in a barrel, and they are small. We do feed them with milk.

Earlier, reference was made to children learning to distinguish between the categories of fiction and non-fiction. Their own writing helps this understanding as they express ideas both in accurate description and imaginatively.

The examples in this chapter are included not because they are considered to be particularly outstanding but as typical writing of children at first school. They demonstrate how at this stage, written verbal expression becomes established as a satisfying medium for children to order, clarify and communicate their ideas and feelings. It is one among many which will be used as is discussed in Chapter 3, but language controls and organizes experience and expression with a precision not possible in other media. It must be emphasized that this expression is concerned with ideas and feelings arising from a child's total interaction with his environment. The term self-expression has been avoided, since it is not a discrete 'self' which is expressed but a person's interpretation and reflection upon his reactions to people and events. Children must have something to talk and to write about if they are not to become inarticulate or illiterate, or to be forced back into fantasy experiences. One of the functions of school is to provide situations which will interest children and therefore provoke thought and emotional involvement. In some areas this is more difficult than others: perhaps a large suburban housing estate is an area most lacking in stimulus, but in all areas the school has a special responsibility for widening the children's experience.

The opportunity to write when an interest and the desire to communicate is at its height will influence the quality of children's writing. If children are required to write at certain times during the day, or every day, they will tend to write the empty and trivial. This is unfortunate for it will not lead to real satisfaction for the writer, and neither will it help him to recognize from his own experience the quality of thought and feeling involved in the writing of the stories and poetry he hears or reads.

It is recognized that few children will as adults become authors or poets, and that, for many, writing will fulfil mainly a practical purpose. However, the world of literature can be available to all as a source of pleasure, reflection and insight. For many children the first real encounter of this world will be in the first school, and this chapter has attempted to explore some of the implications of this encounter. Bantock [3] provides an apt summing-up of the relation of literature to the total educational process:

> The ultimate purpose of education . . . I take to be clarification of the world of nature, of the world of man, and of the internal world of sensation and reflection, of emotion and cognition. Today, that clarification can be achieved by direct experiences and through the accumulated experience of others conveyed through our book culture; we need the fullest possible interaction between the two and this implies a high degree of conscious awareness, of interplay between what is read and what is lived.

CHAPTER 5

Movement: Action, Feeling and Thought

A BABY is born into a world full of movement. He is surrounded by all sorts of activity, including the natural motion of the universe, the mechanical devices of modern living and by human movement itself. A baby's activity at this stage could be said to be undifferentiated, with involvement of the whole body and no observable sign of spatial orientation or personal expression. There is simply an ebbing and flowing of movement seen at its most obvious as going and stopping and this is in complete contrast to the variety, skill and refinement to be found in the movement of the adults around him.

The actions of being picked up, put down, turned over, cuddled and carried about are done to him and for him and eventually will be done by him. Parts of his mother's body will become emphasized: the hands that hold, the arms that rock and the lips that kiss. Impressions will be made on him by the expressive quality with which the body is used and the actions carried out: he will feel the strength and firmness of the lift, the gentleness of the caress and the vitality of the quick and lively facial gestures designed to make him laugh. He comes to recognition of the different rhythms of the people around him as they move: the light, crisp steps of one, the slow, heavy tread of another and the flowing patter of a third. These come to him as distinct dynamic patterns, their rhythms being the individually expressive way that various activities are carried out.

A mother, in her unique relationship with her baby, will often be especially selective in movement in order to convey appropriate expression in voice and bodily gesture. The quiet, soothing, leisurely tone often used may be accompanied by a stroking or rocking, involving the same constituent elements of movement, and this often affects the baby, who first shares the mood actively with his mother and sometimes retains it. In a similar way, the short, brisk and effervescent movement and tone, perhaps used in a time of shared playfulness, produces yet another mood. The establishment of any such moods within the baby is brought about by the imitation of the vocal and bodily activity of the adult. At first this imitation is limited to the availability of the patterns he has already experienced as his own, but it develops until, at about ten months, he is able to imitate things not previously experienced. At this stage he appears to be successful in producing a general mood through imitated activity without adhering to strict bodily detail.

> A boy, ten months, watched an adult shake his arms in the air and laugh in an attempt to excite him. The boy responded, producing the laugh but with a shaking of the head instead of the arms. The mood was recognizably the same, although the shaking action took place in a different part of the body. The expression given to the movement was similar to the adult's, though less refined.

About the same time the baby enjoys the different placing of accent in movement as people play with him. There are many games in which the adult makes a movement which starts some way away from the baby and which travels nearer him, gathering speed and force and culminating in a moment of impact and excitement as he is touched or picked up. Often some vocal sound or word play accompanies this game. When this is repeated sufficiently the baby appears to join in with the activity, almost anticipating the climax at the end. Conversely, the play may start with an accent and fade away, as when the baby is lifted with a strong, quick flourish and lowered slowly and gently. The baby's awareness increases as he sees and listens to his mother, and others close to him, in different situations, moods and relationships.

One of the indications of movement development is an increasing range of actions. At birth the baby has a limited repertoire of unrefined actions at his disposal, which are reflex-like in character and include sucking, crying and grasping. Out of these beginnings grow the sensory-motor actions which typify the first two years. As well as increasing in number these actions begin to be intentionally directed towards people and things and also become co-ordinated with each other.

Many of these early actions involve manipulation but as the baby continues to develop physically an increasing number are concerned with postural control, balance and locomotion. As he sits up, crawls, stands up and walks not only is he adding new actions to his collection but as he can now reach many more things in an increasingly large area of space his active schemata are more extensively brought into play. Once walking is achieved, variations of locomotion appear, running being the first to emerge as a result of increased speed of walking rather than a new action idea. Jumping begins between two and three years, although at first there is very limited activity involving the two feet being used together, usually when the child jumps from a higher to a lower level. At this stage there seems little appreciation of the kind of action which is needed to take the body into the air. Nearly all children can jump by the time they start school but all teachers know the varying degrees of skill that exist among forty children.

Movement development implies not only a larger range but increased skill of action and this comes about partly through repetition. A child climbs more skilfully through climbing more often. Flavell [15] writes of repetition being one of the main attributes of assimilation and mentions 'the intrinsic tendency to reach out into the environment again and again and incorporate what it can'. The child also increases his skill by climbing in different situations where he has to adapt, for example, to changing surfaces, heights, widths and angles. Refinement of movement, seen as part of increasing skill, calls for a certain selection. At two years of age a child will negotiate an obstacle by making a wide, sweeping curve, while a four-year-old not only has the ability to manoeuvre his body more accurately but also knows more about where in space, and when in time, to direct his steps. Comparative observations were made between different age groups in a situation demanding refinement of this sort:

> A two-year-old boy, feeding ducks, had difficulty in the release action of his hand, of letting the bread go at the right moment. After the throw his fingers remained extended for a long time,

even as the hand returned to take hold of more bread. Nor had
he developed the finer finger movement necessary to break
the bread into smaller pieces.

A six-year-old girl showed much greater ability to eliminate
unnecessary movement in a similar operation, merging the
separate stages into a whole through harmonious, bodily, effort
and spatial transitions. She looked much more practised and
skilful.

The child's increasing ability to be economical in movement
is partly due to a greater understanding of height, weight,
distance and depth, etc. The handling and manipulation of
objects involved in carrying out his purposes improves efficiency
of movement in a way that no amount of copying can do. It
appears that smaller movements take longer to become refined
than larger actions and doing up buttons and belts where
finger manipulation and small spatial pattern plays a significant
part, may not be completely within the range of all five-year-
olds when they encounter school for the first time.

Another feature of movement development is that of appropriateness and this has two aspects. First there is the appropriateness of the type of action used for a functional task and this
needs little explanation. For example, when a five-year-old
starts school we accept that he will use a turning action to
unscrew a top from a bottle or a piercing action to produce a
hole in the carton of milk so that the straw will go in. A much
younger child will simply tug and pull at the top that needs
unscrewing and not know how to make the hole for the straw.
But appropriateness refers not only to the action itself but to its
nature and quality. The action of catching will have to be
gentle if the soap bubble is to remain intact, quick if the
falling leaf is to be captured; the throw must be hard if it is to
make a big splash in the pool and hard, too, must be the unscrewing action on the obstinate bottle top. Movement of an
expressive kind, arising from inner feeling rather than outer
need, also increases in appropriateness. Graphic descriptions
in movement develop from large gestures of general meaning
in the very young child to a more detailed and specifically
appropriate form with older ones. For example, in using
descriptive gestures to illustrate the story of the three bears, a

Plate 2   Boy, 4 yrs. 'Rocket.'

Plate 3   Boy, 4 yrs. 'Me on my bicycle.'

Plate 4   Boy, 5 yrs. 'A rabbit.'

Plate 5   Girl, 6 yrs. 'An elephant.'

Plate 6 Girl, 5 yrs. 'Deer.'

Plate 7 Girl, 5 yrs. 'Cat and dog and horse.'

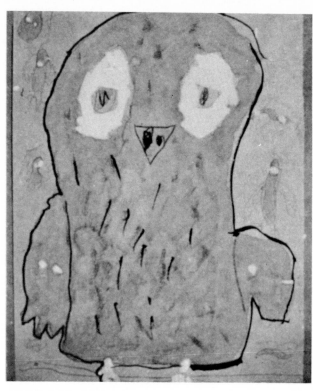

Plate 8 Boy, 6 yrs. 'Owl.'

Plate 9 Boy, 7 yrs. 'St. George.'

Plate *10*   Boy, 8 yrs. 'Horses.'

Plate *11*   Boy, 5 yrs.

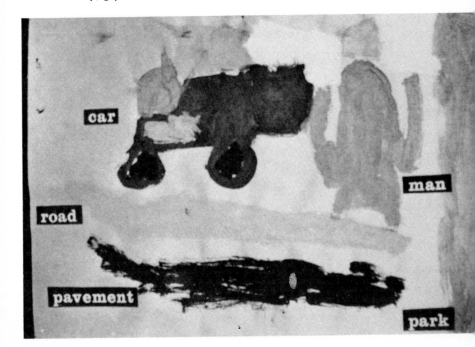

Plate *12*   Girl, 6 yrs. 'Riding in a bus.'

Plate *13*   Boy, 6 yrs. 'Men on horse-back.'

Plate *14*   Girl, 7 yrs. 'Our boat trip under Tower Bridge.'

Plate *15*   Boy, 6 yrs. 'Train.'

Plate 16 Boy, 6 yrs.

Plate 17 Boy, 6 yrs. 'Peter had German measles and it is catching.'

Plate 18 Exploring environment through movement.

Plate 19 'It's higher now, it's too high to jump, there's further to drop.'

Plate 20 (also *21, 22, 23*) Arms are brought into play to help in unusual feats of balancing.

Plate 21

Plate 22

Plate 23

Plate 24 (also *25*)   The 'thinking body' in action.

Plate 25

Plate 26 (also *27*)   Problem solving: In their efforts to travel along the peg ladder, two children respond differently to the structure of the apparatus.

Plate 27

Plate 28 Individual response of the five-year-olds.

Plate 29 Two seven-year-olds engaged in a partner activity, showing a decrease of egocentricity.

Plate 30 (also *31*)   Dancing in the air and on the ground.

Plate 31

six-year-old will express not only the height of the three chairs Goldilocks sat on but also the different qualities of the movement with which she approached them and reacted to their size, comfort and durability. The four-year-old will be less concerned about the expression matching the situation and the movement will be less telling. In the home corner, as the child works out the situations in which he is involved, he chooses appropriate movement qualities to differentiate father from baby brother or the teacher. This demands selection which in turn calls for a wide range of effort and as this increases he is able to be even more specifically appropriate—for example, portraying father in a kind, or in an angry, mood. Children also need to be appropriate in the expression of their own moods and relationships. They soon learn that no-one is going to believe that they wish to be friends if their overtures are aggressive or domineering.

Children have a natural appetite for movement and need to move as they need to eat and sleep. The physical need to move frequently and with differentiation, and the associated psychological need to examine what is possible at the existing stage, was referred to in the Introduction and the depth of such need to move is made apparent, on the one hand, by a study of those who have been deprived and, on the other, by a study of those with every opportunity. Within the overall appetite there are particular areas of movement which children naturally seek for themselves and it is the recognition of these areas which should lead to the provision of movement opportunities in our schools, the pre-school and out-of-school activities providing the take-over point for extended and structured learning.

One such type of activity is that related directly to the physical environment, through which children gain experience, knowledge and understanding both of their immediate surroundings and of themselves. For example, they climb trees, railings and fences, balance along walls and kerbstones, swing round lampposts and overhanging branches, somersault over bus barriers and jump on, off and over anything in sight.

Most L.E.A.'s recognize the need of young children for this kind of agility experience and large apparatus is provided in the majority of our infants' schools. If the apparatus and space are sufficient the children need to be left free for some of the time to work on their own, to start, stop, change and rest as they choose and as indeed they would if the climbing frames were the trees outside, the pole were the narrow wall around the public library and the box the pile of bricks at the end of the garden used to jump off again and again. Their being unguided for a while does not result in lack of activity, on the contrary everyone appears to carry out even the simplest tasks with a sense of purpose, and the overall activity at the beginning is intense and vital although, within this intensity, individual children may be resting and cogitating as part of the lesson. At this stage suggestions from the teacher come most naturally from looking at and talking with individual children who are working at their self-chosen activity, and here the teacher will try to bring the understanding involved in the activity to a more conscious level. She attempts not only to increase the movement content but also the resulting verbal exchange. As the first full-bodied attack subsides, the children are often ready for the teacher's contribution and, in this respect, the rhythmic pattern of activity within this type of agility lesson seems similar to that in the classroom at the beginning of the day and described in Chapter 10.

With this natural turning of the children to the teacher, and with such large numbers working at once, it is sometimes appropriate to give general comment, help and encouragement. Suggestions encouraging movement exploration should be general enough for each child to use, if he is ready to do so, as forty children are likely to be doing and needing to do different things at the same time. The young child is very concerned with his own body and one of the most suitable areas of exploration is through the play of different body parts and through bodily action. Teachers could lead the children to experiment, for example, with the actions of jumping, swinging, climbing and balancing, perhaps through combining them in some way or finding out how they vary on different pieces of apparatus. In the case of young infants, they need to be helped towards an awareness of the body parts used by an association of names. How often has a reception class been unresponsive to a teacher's suggestions because the children do not know the name of the part of the body being referred to? To mention knees, feet, hands and ankles as they move on apparatus will help this awareness and suggest activity. Work which is still quite general at five becomes rather more specific towards the top of the infants' school. The five-year-old's activity may be random or suggested by the perceptual features of the environment: the seven-year-old's activity has intention and he does something particular. Some seven-year-olds can see several ways of achieving what they have set out to do, and the teacher can play an important role, showing two children carrying out a similar activity in different ways. A few older infants can think about their activity without doing it and are able to plan modifications.

If a harmonious development has taken place during the early years there is a freedom and unhamperedness about the body of a young boy or girl that is at its height in the primary school, and it is no wonder that small children spend so much time trying out their bodies in feats of strength, invention, dexterity and daring. If we need to renew our faith in this established truth we need only to wander in a park on a summer's day to see children at play working out these feats. By five a child is secure in maintaining his upright stance and is able to regain his balance at will, and he now begins to experiment widely, with increasingly difficult acts involving an acrobatic and mobile use of his body. He enjoys rolling down grassy slopes, trying to stand on his head and his hands, to crab-walk upside down and on all fours, to jump high in the air or far across the ground and to use his feet in a variety of nimble ways. Entirely self-motivated, this play involves finding possible activities and then practising over and over again. How many times may a child put his hands on the floor and kick up his feet behind him in order to achieve that much longed for, single moment of inverted balance? Some children will need to try hundreds of times perhaps but each attempt will tell them something more about the nature of support, the distribution of the weight of the body, the alignment of the body and the timing involved. And it is the relatedness of these pieces of learning which eventually brings about the desired success.

To follow up this type of activity, and to cater for this aspect of children's movement, many schools include on their timetables lessons which may be called 'agility work on the floor', or 'movement leading to gymnastics'. Although this activity belongs to a different category from work related to apparatus some teachers provide for this at the beginning of a period before children use the apparatus which is already out. However, other teachers prefer to take this work in a separate session in a space free from apparatus. Working without the apparatus allows greater freedom of thought for the teacher too, in her efforts to help the children form and clarify ideas. So often in order to make use of the situation when the apparatus is out the children have been asked to transfer the floor movements to work on the apparatus. This is an unrealistic task, for the children are unlikely to be able to adapt the type of activity worked out in the hall to the structure of the apparatus. What a six-year-old chooses to do with unlimited space around him is not likely to be appropriate anywhere else. The two situations demand different sorts of problem solving and it is only at a much later stage of development that a child is able to abstract the principles concerned and would manage and enjoy such a challenge.

Again during this sort of activity the teacher can help the children to think more consciously through their bodies and extend their learning. Tasks and challenges should be general where each child is able to find a personal reply in movement. Agility on the floor appears to be of three main kinds; movement which goes on to the floor and the weight of the body is taken in different ways, movement which travels across the floor, involving a variety of ways of locomotion and that which takes the body away from the floor and into the air, with all sorts of jumps. Broad considerations such as these could suggest a variety of suitable tasks as well as providing a check for overall development. Emphasizing the use or non-use of body parts will bring further possibilities into focus and will ensure that everyone can find a special way of moving. After such general exploration older infants may then be encouraged to make up a sequence, for example, moving on the feet, then for a time moving without using them and then finding an appropriate ending. In this way they are helped to establish individual phrases of movement which are their own and which may be repeated. It is important that these can then be shown at any time to be appreciated and discussed as would be their clay models, paintings or stories. Much of the work in movement in the first school is towards variety and invention but skill has its place here and comes as a result of the repetition of purposeful activity. But we must be careful to aim at general skilfulness and not at specific skills imposed on the children. In other words while it is inappropriate to teach a class of such young children to do handstands, it would be a good thing to get them involved in learning to take weight on different parts of their bodies, including their hands. In this way skilfulness and variety go hand in hand, each making demands from the other in a bid for excitement and satisfaction. The children will invent different sequences of movement and will enjoy discovering their bodily powers and capabilities.

As well as experiencing their surroundings through movement and exploring their bodies acrobatically, children also enjoy handling objects and making them move. Throwing pebbles into the sea, kicking a stone and beating a stick against a wall are just a few examples which come into this category.

In most schools this type of activity is catered for by the provision of small apparatus, in the form of bats, balls, ropes and hoops. Although experience of games should not be precluded it would seem more appropriate for the youngest infants simply to have such apparatus available to use how and when they choose. The wide differences in physical abilities in children of this age, combined with incomplete co-ordination and concepts of space and time make it essentially a stage for playing with the material. In their own natural play with objects previously mentioned, a lot of time is spent in doing the same thing over and over again without moving on to more complex activities, yet it does not seem to be practising for perfection. The pebble continues for some time just to be thrown into the sea before it is aimed at a piece of driftwood or made to skim. At about the age of seven one can expect a more extensive readiness to learn and the children enjoy finding out how high the ball will bounce with a certain force, where to aim for it to go through a certain hole, in fact how the thinking body must act for the material to behave in a certain way. Through the handling of the different size, weight, length and shape of these materials children are learning to estimate, adapt and respond through movement. 'How long', 'how high', 'how many' and 'how far' are a few of the phrases which arise in the play of the young child as he makes the hoops, balls and ropes move, and is, in turn, moved by them.

Since among other things five- and six-year-olds are not always ready to cope with the complexities of independently moving apparatus, they are rarely seen playing games with apparatus and other people of their own age. Where these games do happen they are usually found to be organized and kept going by older companions. Perhaps we have been slow to recognize this, or perhaps the tradition of British gamesmanship is so strong that we cannot wait to foster it, but it is true to say that some schools believe in a very early introduction to games. However, as teachers try to exploit the early tendencies to play together, hopefully trying partner and small group work, they will realize the limitations and frustrations of such externally organized play in which these very young children cannot manage moving apparatus in relation to other people. But at the end of the first school there will be some working alongside each other in a mutual way, which may be utilized, and which Piaget [39] calls the stage of incipient co-operation. Rules, if they exist at all, are few and made only when the situation of the moment demands. But because they are self-made and appropriately related to the game in progress, they are understood by the children concerned, incidentally providing the best basis for major games such as netball and football when they are most appropriately introduced at the top of the junior school.

Sometimes in their play children choose to engage in movement for its own sake and to use it expressively. In a young child some of the first things to be noticed are the spontaneous outbreaks of rhythmic activity, the waving, beating and shaking of arms: the leaping, whirling, swirling, swooping and being still. He shows the anger he feels when his toys are taken, the tenderness when looking after a patient in the home corner and excitement can make him shiver or gesticulate explosively. Unstylized, often unrepeated, this is not dance but is certainly the stuff of dance. We see signs of dance too as children spin together for the sheer enjoyment of the sensation of movement. Or we may see it in the spontaneous activity of a child moving unobserved to the radio or in front of a mirror and in the piece of dramatic play when a boy puts on a helmet, picks up a sword and 'becomes' a soldier. Children express ideas, moods, feelings and relationships through movement, and through movement respond to the world of motion and so identify themselves with life and living.

How then does the teacher begin to incorporate these things into her work so that she can give the children a dance experience? For here there are no boxes or bars, no bats or balls, no stunt-like activities, just the children, the space and herself. The primary source of dance for young children is surely movement itself of the kind they use when they jump, bounce, spin, go, stop, sway and swirl. The teacher may help the extension of such ideas so that the children create a spinning and running dance or a punching and stamping dance. Sometimes she may work on one or two of these phrases with all the class who respond in their own way to the common challenge, and sometimes she may help them to establish an independently motivated phrase. Young children, when pursuing their own phrases, often go on, ad infinitum, so that spinning and turning are experimented with but little attention is paid to beginning and end. This is as it should be, but in order to help their understanding of phrasing the teacher may sometimes choose to use an action phrase which has a definite end, such as 'creeping, creeping, spinning and stop' or 'shiver and freeze'. This does not mean that all the children do identical movements; variety can be encouraged within the sequence so that spinning may be carried out on different parts of the body, and creeping may be low down, high up, forwards or sideways. Shivering may occur in different areas of the body or all over and the 'freezing' may result in unusual body shapes. In making up such phrases herself the teacher helps the children's sense of wholeness just as she does in story or song. Gradually, however, by sharing with the teacher as well as through their own efforts, the children begin to create their own sequences which can either end or be repeated. The following two phrases and accompanying comment show such development:

> Girl, 6 years: Sway and swirl and fall on the ground. (Each time she did this it came to an end and there was a break before it was repeated.)

Boy, 7 years: I'm jerking, and jumping, I'm flying through the
air. (Repeated several times continuously.)
Comment: 'Yours gets dead, mine goes on and on.'

Movement may be considered as the primary source of dance-
like activity, but things that can be touched, heard and seen
are also excellent and readily obtainable starting points for
dance. Touching, itself a form of movement, is essentially an
action imbued with expressive quality and often accompanied
by a tone of voice coloured with similar expression. Both depend to some extent on the nature of the object or material
touched. One is aware of the sudden, sharp withdrawal from
something hot or spiky, the gentle, lingering sensation when
fur is stroked, the sensitive, flexible movement of trying to
catch a bubble and the firm, resolute action in playing a
resounding rhythm on a drum, or tearing a piece of card. Such
tactile stimuli provide a good starting point and one which the
children readily enjoy. When handling a horse-chestnut, the
children will touch and see the sharp, prickly outer case and, in
contrast, the smooth curve of the conker inside and such an
experience may well be taken into dance where spiky and
smooth movements may be explored.

Sometimes what is heard can stimulate dance and the
children may rush and roar just as the wind has been rushing
and roaring in the playground, expressing the essence of the
freely flowing wind, the strong and sudden gusts and the light,
playful breezes in between. Or the sound they hear and respond
to may come about as they move with percussion instruments
and signs of this will have been noticed at the music table. The
sounds of the various instruments suggest different qualities
of movement so that the children and their instruments can
'speak' in several tones. They may also move in response to a
sound sequence provided by the teacher and here she will
have particular themes in mind to help increase their language
of movement expression. Music is also a possible starting point
for this group of aural stimuli, but one which should be used
sparingly with young children when they are busy establishing
their own personal rhythms and find it difficult to conform to
such highly structured sound not of their own making. However, some short, complete pieces, some especially written for

dance with infants, may well be used with discretion, often with exciting results.

What can be seen around them can serve as a basis for dance too; the machines in the boiler house, the clock on the interest table, the shadows which are always there while the sun is out, the fish that dart around in the tank and the fireworks let off the previous evening.

There are many such starting points which the teacher may use with the children, too many to list here, and many of which have their beginning in the classroom. Often as they respond to the varied provision around them dance-like ideas emerge and become the foundation for yet another creative activity alongside clay, water, sand and collage. Through the observations of such beginnings the teacher gradually selects certain general experiences which she could develop to advantage in the larger space in the hall. In order to help the children extend their understanding the teacher may emphasise various aspects of movement appropriate to the ideas being used.

Movement can be impressive upon the individual as well as expressive of him and part of the teacher's role is therefore to provide opportunities for the children to assimilate movement patterns so that an inner enrichment takes place which itself aids expression. Therefore, during any dance lesson, as well as giving opportunities for the expressive aspect of movement, the teacher may organize movement situations where the children use latent qualities, less frequently used spatial ideas or unusual bodily co-ordinations and actions. In this way, as in all the other ways, she will be helping them to develop the language of movement and to speak clearly, fluently and with meaning.

If we accept the value of movement as essential activity, then we must also see that some classification of movement is necessary in order to recognize the special stresses within the children's own responses and, as teachers, to enable us to be selective in the help we are able to give.

It is obvious from what we see and do that the body is the central core of human movement. For the child, it is an instrument with a rapidly increasing range of movement possibilities: it is a tool constantly in use, exploring and acting upon the environment in an effort to establish self; it is also the instrument of immediate experience. The young infant is still learning about the different parts of the body used in action and giving them names, and is establishing areas like top and bottom halves, and right and left sides. The junior child is able to use his body in a more detailed way and with greater differentiation.

In movement the medium is space—the space immediately around the body, known as the *kinesphere*, and the space beyond which is shared by the individual and others. Concentration on space is made apparent by the use of simple directions, patterns and pathways on the floor and in the air, the shape of the body in space and the size and extension of movement.

Just as all movement takes place in space, so all movement has an expressive nature. This expression is appreciated through special colours or tones, known as 'effort' involving quality of movement, which is an external manifestation of an inner state: it is this expression that causes us to recognize individuals and to acknowledge individuality. All children have a potentially wide range of movement expression, while showing preferred areas that they use more frequently. We may recognize in a particular child a love of sudden and forceful movements but, at the same time, acknowledge his ability to express gentle and leisurely movement, if and when the occasion demands. It is this rich range that we must stimulate and foster if he is to learn to select appropriately.

In the establishment of concepts and learning patterns generally, the key, of course, is relationship. Relatedness in movement is important, starting with the relationship of body parts one to another, the relationship of one area of movement to another and the relationship of body to different objects, leading to the development of sound personal relationships within the context of the primary school. In learning to relate in these various ways, the child is learning an awareness of self through doing; he is extending this concept by relating himself to himself, to space, to the teacher and to other children —all in increasing complexity. All children move. It is our job to help them to raise this activity to a higher conscious level.

Dance, agility work on and off apparatus, play with bats and balls are thoughtfully and well established within the schools but although these named areas exist, the line between them is faint, and we should be careful not to let our own categorization hamper the children. With young children the work will be very general and it will not always be easy to separate the different modes of movement and expression. With young children much of the work could be called 'movement play', through which they explore the body's capacity for activity.

It is important to recognize the role of movement as a common denominator of the total development of the child, and its integrating function. Movement is bound up with physical, intellectual and emotional development and a child's doing, thinking and feeling may be examined in movement terms.

The relatedness of movement and physical development is obvious through the growing child's increasing ability to manage the weight, height, length and proportions of his body. It is important to note that the relationship of these bodily characteristics is constantly in a state of change. Control of the body in a variety of ways in response to environmental challenges is one aspect of the increasing skill evident in this respect.

To illustrate this point it may be helpful to look at the way a baby behaves in his initial attempts to stand alone, noticing the wide base used. The arms, previously used to hold on to people and things, still remain away from the sides of the body and are now used in a mobile way to maintain balance. As proficiency in standing erect is increased the balancing role of the arms is reduced and eventually eliminated. But through a continuing exploration of the environment similar bodily responses may be called for again and arms come into play once more, for example, as mobility of balance is demanded from the seven-year-old trying to balance on a narrow ledge. Such patterns of behaviour continue to come into play when new situations demand unusual balancing skills such as walking on icy roads, and it is interesting to follow this through to adult specialist occupations and see similar bodily adjustment in the tight rope walker and the steward at sea.

Another example of related development of this sort may be seen in the attempts of two and three-year-olds to catch a ball. Their hands are held in an almost passive way, as if to receive rather than to take hold of it. At this stage a child cannot actively catch a ball because the eyes do not yet work together and there is an undeveloped sense of depth and distance. Also lacking is the muscular control and co-ordination necessary to carry out such an action. Maturation at this stage is an important factor in learning, practice assuming greater importance later.

The relatedness of movement and intellectual development may be appreciated in the ways in which a child's body comes into contact with the environment in an active way and through which he is able to judge depths, heights, distances and lengths.

> A group of five-year-olds were jumping off a plank which they were using in conjunction with a climbing frame. At intervals they dismantled the plank and moved it to a higher level. As the height increased children dropped out of the game with varying reactions. At one stage a boy walked to the end, looked down and said, 'It's higher now, it's too high to jump, there's further to drop.'

Through trying out jumps from different heights and experiencing different lengths of drop, he could now estimate that from a certain height the distance to fall would be too much for him to attempt. As indicated in the Introduction, the boy was basing his estimation, not on guesswork, but on a frame of reference built up through his activity. Another aspect of learning through doing is seen in the following example:

> Two children, aged seven and four, playing on a see-saw, found that the inequality of their weight affected the act of balancing. Through experimentation they found that although the lack of weight of the one prevented that end of the see-saw descending, this could be overcome to a certain extent by an increased push-off by the bigger child.

It may be clearly seen that the older child accommodated to the situation as he met it and modified his resulting behaviour.

> A five-year-old boy climbed up, down and across the net many times before he verbalized his activity and subsequent interest in the number seven. The highest point to which he dared climb, counted by himself and his friends, was the seventh rung which he thought about in several ways expressed through phrases such as 'Two more to go', 'Nearly there', 'Not far off' and 'I can't manage the last one'.

In these examples of children thinking through movement the
body was in motion while the material was relatively stable and
a separate entity. Because of this particular type of relationship
specific rhythmic and spatial patterns of movement arise which,
prompted by exploration, are consolidated by repetition.
Evidence is also at hand when children handle objects and play
with them.

> Two boys aged six and nine playing with sticks were engaged
> in a sword fight, the younger one coming off badly and never
> scoring a hit. He remarked that his opponent's arm was longer
> than his and suggested that he should therefore have a shorter
> sword.

These comments reflected his thinking, first the acceptance of
the length of his friend's arm as an unalterable fact but then
an adjustment of the situation in his favour. Such thinking
had taken place while the game was in progress and this is
similarly exemplified in the solitary play going on in the next
example:

> A six-year-old boy was playing with his bow and arrow. He
> found that if he aimed into the air the arrow landed close to
> him while a straighter, more horizontally directed shot meant a
> more distant landing. Following this initial discovery concern-
> ing cause and effect he went on to experiment with other factors
> determining the arrow's flight such as the angle of aim, the
> degree of focus and the kind of tension in drawing the bow.

A decrease in egocentricity is characteristic of intellectual
development in children between five and eight and this increasing ability to give, take and put oneself into another's
position is often seen in movement sessions.

> Groups of eight-year-old girls who were dancing about like
> witches were asked to finish in a group together. Each time
> they tried, a muddle occurred and while they rested from
> their efforts they planned their next attempt. 'You stop lower,
> then I'll come in on top' was the first comment. Then 'You
> get there first, then I'll know where to go.'

Here is an illustration of thought as internalized action involving the ability to go back to the beginning.

Movement is as clearly related to emotional as to physical

and intellectual development. Jumping for joy, shaking with fear or excitement and standing in awe literally happen to young children. They express such feelings fully and freely, whereas in the adult the action may be minimized, reduced or controlled. The latter does not need to perform such large scale movement and often internalizes the action completely.

Before speech is present, movement communicates by itself and there is an action stress; secondly comes a time when words and movement are interchangeable languages, with words colouring movement or movement adding description to speech. Finally speech becomes the primary means of emotional communication and expression, with movement playing a secondary part. It is noticeable in adults, however, that behaviour is variable at this third stage, and while some show economy of gesture and almost imperceptible movements which shadow their main actions, others appear to gain verbal fluency through accompanying motion.

Movement, however small, is a means of expressing and communicating and children show themselves as unique individuals through their self-chosen patterns of movement. This expression is observable when descriptive gestures are used and also in utilitarian tasks such as moving a chair or picking up a pencil. Allport [1] in a definition of expression refers to 'the style of behaving' and talks of expressive movement as 'one's manner of performing adaptive acts'. Laban [27], too, says that all movement is expressive, even the most functional, and both Allport and Laban stress the 'how' rather than the 'what' of movement in this context.

In his concept of 'effort' Laban put forward the idea that a personal attitude towards the motion factors of weight, space, time and flow result in qualitative movement which may be observed in people and by which they may be recognized. We can distinguish children who move predominantly with gentleness and sensitivity (fine touch) and those whose movement shows strength and power (firmness). Similarly we can see children who are outgoing (free flow) or those who hold back a little (bound flow), those who are hasty and urgent (suddenness) and those more leisurely in manner (sustainment). And there are some who appear to prefer a threadlike channelling of attention (directness) to a more extensive plasticity (flexibility).

Each individual builds up a personal repertoire made up of varying kinds of such effort qualities and combinations with others which expresses his style of doing things and establishes an image for others. Every child will have a different way, for example, of opening a door, coming into a room and sitting down and we say that this is typical of him. Certainly from an early age each child has a personal movement make-up and his behaviour is distinguishable by a preferred and unique mode of expression. It is probably this that enables one to recognize friends at a great distance before their features can be discerned. However, although certain factors remain constant within one's movement make-up, others change according to situation and occasion. As well as individual shapes and rhythms there are certain general dynamic forms and patterns common to most children in the expression of moods such as anger, excitement, hilarity and distress.

Action can precipitate feeling or alternatively, feeling can result in action, and in the young child usually does. The reader may well be able to remember a young child clapping hands and jumping up and down at the prospect of a particularly enjoyable treat. (See Dr. Blurton Jones [6]. The ethologists may eventually have much to contribute to our observations in this area.) Excitement is conveyed by something in addition to the actions of jumping and clapping themselves and this is the personal style in which they are performed. The process can, as indicated, happen in reverse with action promoting feeling. Again a familiar situation may be recalled where children begin to chase each other round and round in a circle, and as the game goes on the purposefulness of the chasing decreases, bodily precision diminishes and a hilarious, uncontrolled situation arises. It is a pattern frequently seen and adults experienced in such play times may be heard to warn: 'Stop that or you'll get over-excited.' Indeed such a situation may well end in tears.

Action may also modify feeling:

A six-year-old who had lost his temper ran out of the house to his bicycle. He rode up and down, making each turn as noisy and spectacular as possible but, after a time when no-one had objected, he became interested in the turning process itself and engrossed in the variety of stunts which emerged as he experimented.

These required intricate moments of balance and timing, very different mood constituents from the furious pedalling and unthinking turning with which he had started, although these still played a part. Through a whole series of actions a very different mood had come about and great satisfaction was felt. Opportunities for mood modification through movement would seem to be something that should be readily available in the infants' school.

These recent examples of mood expression and mood modification through movement and those related to physical and intellectual development illustrate the need for children to move as part of their total development while those quoted earlier showed a need for movement in its own right and as specialized activity. Nevertheless, however movement is viewed it remains a visible expression of the wholeness of life since movement is indivisible from life. This not only applies to the utilitarian aspect of living but because of the fact that every movement of man is expressive of himself, his aims, struggles and achievements, it reflects the inner activity of the person. For these reasons alone we should satisfy the movement appetite of the young children in our schools.

CHAPTER 6

Mathematics: Ordering, Relating, Measuring

'MATHEMATICS is based on experience; it is the crystallization of relationships into a beautifully regular structure, distilled from our actual contacts with the real world.' (Z. P. Dienes, *Building Up Mathematics*, Hutchinson, 1960.)

The contacts with the world to which Dienes refers begin at birth. Although it will be some five years or so before the crystallization of these relationships into the structure of mathematics is clearly apparent, this process can be seen in early childhood. The genesis of mathematical concepts lies in the earliest explorations of infancy, as a baby discovers the permanence of objects, spatial continuity, and sequence in his own actions and in events which happen to him. The learning which results from these early explorations is on the plane of practical intelligence, and although it may be established at this level by eighteen months to two years, it will take another three to five years for it to be established on the plane of thought. For example, up to approximately eight months a feeding bottle exists for a baby only in terms of his own actions. If, when hungry, he can see the bottle he will show signs of excitement at the prospect of food, but if the bottle is removed from his vision, the anticipatory behaviour ceases, and he does not search for it. This would indicate his unawareness of its existence outside the space he perceives. Similarly if the bottle is presented with the nipple towards him he will recognize it, but if the reverse end is presented he may show no signs of recognition, nor will it occur to him to move his body to obtain a different view. Gradually, however, he begins to move his body and objects in space in order to obtain different points of view so that eventually he can search for a bottle after it has been displaced under several different covers, and not only turn it so that the nipple is towards him, but also tilt it at an angle to make it possible for the liquid to reach his mouth. This he understands in terms of his own sensory-motor actions: he has learned what he must do in order to obtain the liquid, but he is not of course consciously aware of the spatial relationship of the liquid to the bottle.

In a series of experiments, Piaget [44] has shown the slow development of this aspect of children's understanding of space. If asked to draw the position of liquid in bottles tilted at various angles, young children up to an age of approximately five years are able to show only the topological understanding of 'surrounding':

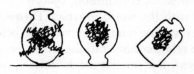

Thus the liquid is shown within the bottle, but there is no notion of the horizontal plane.

At a later stage the plane surface of the liquid is recognized, but that this is always horizontal is not understood:

It is not until later again that on the level of thought it is understood that the plane surface of liquid remains horizontal at whatever angle a bottle is tilted and that this can be represented accurately in drawing. Most children do not reach this stage until approximately seven years of age, and for some it may be even later.

The slow development of mathematical ideas as illustrated in this example of the concept of space can also be seen in the building up of the concept of conservation. In the mathematical sense conservation involves the understanding that, if nothing is added or subtracted, quantity has not changed in spite of any variety of transformations. Quantity here refers both to continuous quantity, for example, sand, flour, water, and to discontinuous quantity, i.e. discrete objects such as bricks, dolls, etc.

The origins of the understanding of conservation lie in a baby's discovery of the permanence of the object. In the previous example the cessation of the baby's activity when the bottle was removed from his vision not only illustrates his lack of spatial awareness, but also indicates that for him it exists only in his own actions, in his looking, smelling and feeling. Gradually, objects begin to acquire a permanent existence for him, but at first this is perceived through extensions in his own actions. For example, a toy he drops over the side of a pram can still be seen although it cannot be felt, or if he is stretching for a toy at the moment it is being hidden under a cover, he will continue to stretch and pull the cover to obtain it. By the middle of the second year most babies know that an object still exists even after several hidden displacements: for example, a doll can be found after being successively hidden under several cushions. The relationship can clearly be seen between the development of ideas of space and of object permanence and in both it is the level of sensory-motor intelligence which is reached during the second year.

At this stage, while the object is understood to exist outside the actions of the child, mathematical attributes and relationships are not perceived. A group of objects can be more or less depending on the space covered, or are anticipated to be heavy or light according to size. Children's drawings and paintings can illustrate these inconsistencies: a person may have five fingers on one hand and eight on the other, or a clothes line may be drawn higher than the roof of the house. Such inconsistencies have been demonstrated by experiments carried out by Piaget [41]. In one of these a child is shown an equal number of eggs and egg-cups. Most children of about five years of age can match egg to cup and agree that they are equal

groups. However if the eggs are spread out then there are
'more eggs', and similarly with the cups. Again, children at
this stage can agree that the amount of liquid in two identical
containers is equal, but if the liquid from one is poured into
four smaller containers or a taller, thinner container then they
think there is 'more' or if it is poured into a shallow, wider
container there is 'not so much'. In a further example children
are presented with two sticks which they agree are equal in
length. However, if one is moved beyond the end of the other,
this is said to be 'longer' and the other 'shorter'.

Responses of this kind which are typical of younger or less
able children demonstrate lack of conservation; quantity for
them is dependent on perceptual factors and is judged as more
or less according to its appearance. With older or more intelligent children, however, the position changes. Quantity
is conserved, and they therefore understand that it remains
constant in spite of displacements and transformations. They
make comments of which the following is typical:

> Of course they are the same. You didn't take any away or put
> any more there, so they must be the same.

The inference is that the adult is stupid not to be aware of this.

> On one occasion when an adult was pressing a child to confirm
> his conclusion that two new, unsharpened pencils were of
> equal length however arranged, she asked '*Could* you make this
> one shorter than that?' The child replied, 'Yes!'—and was
> only just prevented from breaking it into two pieces!

The discussion so far has been mainly concerned with the
difference between pre-operational and concrete operational
thought. The former is dominated by perceptual factors which
cause a child to focus on particular features in a situation to the
exclusion of other, perhaps more relevant, features. Thus in
the test with eggs and cups, children at this stage centre on the
space covered by the objects and not on the number of objects.
Or, in the experiments with the sticks, the emphasis is on the
differences of the positions of the extremities and not on the
sticks themselves. Understanding at this stage is both inflexible

because it is tied to specific discrete perceptions, and fluctuating since the perceptions can shift. This results in the inconsistencies and contradictions previously described, and is illustrated in the following example of a child, just five, travelling by train to London:

> Some ten minutes after the train left, it stopped at a station and he asked, 'Is this London?' His mother replied that it was not, that London was a long way and it would take a long time to get there—it would not be the next station, nor the next, but the one after that. The child repeated, 'Not the next one, not the next one, but the one after that.' However, when it stopped he again asked, 'Is this London?' and in spite of further and apparently understood explanation, this was repeated at the next station, and again when London was finally reached.

In this example the child's mind was centred on London/ station, thus careful and appropriate explanation did not enable him to consider sequence, distance or time.

It is interesting to compare the thinking of this child with the following example of a boy, just seven, who had been describing a car journey in which he had said that it was eight miles from town A to town B.

> A little later he returned to the teacher and said, 'Well, actually I was wrong. It's not eight miles to B. It's eight miles from C to B. Because we were in A which is one mile from C, and it said "B – 9 miles". So B must be eight miles from C.'

This is an example of concrete operational thinking in which the child is no longer tied to action and perception. It demonstrates the existence of a stable mental structure which enables him to hold the three towns in a conserved, spatial relationship, which is expressed in terms of a standard unit of measurement, the mile. Further, there is mobility within this stable structure, so that he can move in thought backwards and forwards between the three towns and so correct his previous inaccurate statement. This movement back in thought to an original starting point is termed reversibility and is, of course, only possible if beginning and end points can be held in a constant relationship—i.e. if conservation has been achieved.

A seven-year-old girl demonstrated both concepts when she decided to make herself a skirt. With the help of another child she measured herself, then made a paper pattern and followed this by selecting a piece of material which would be large enough. She cut out the skirt, allowing for turnings and hem, then sewed it together and added fastenings, making a garment which it was possible to wear. A girl in another class who was nearly eight years old showed pre-operational thinking in a similar situation. She was making a dress for her doll and wanted to turn up the hem. She pinned it up and tried it on the doll, but decided it was too long. She turned it inside out, unpinned the hem and let it down, thus shortening the hem but lengthening the dress. She was very surprised and puzzled when she tried it on again to find it longer and it was only after discussion with the teacher that she realized and corrected her mistake.

The development of the concept of seriation is another aspect of children's thinking, both mathematical and logical, which Piaget has described. Seriation is concerned with asymmetrical relations, i.e. the ordering of a class of objects in terms of differences in some given attribute, the differences going in a specific direction; for example, $A < B < C < D$ therefore $D > C > B > A$. Piaget has demonstrated this in a variety of experiments. In one of these, which also introduces the notions of cardinal and ordinal numbers, the children were given ten sticks of varying length and were asked to arrange these in order from shortest to longest. When this was done they were given, one at a time, nine more sticks also of varying lengths which they were asked to insert at the correct positions. Later a doll was placed on one of the 'steps' and the children asked how many it had climbed and how many more it had to go to the top. Finally the whole series was disarranged, the doll was placed on one stick and the question repeated. To answer this therefore involved either actually or mentally reconstructing the whole series.

The responses of the youngest children were global and perceptual, demonstrating the features of pre-operational thought already discussed. They could distinguish the longest from the shortest, but were quite unable to organize those in between. At the next stage they could arrange the original series but this was at a perceptual level of 'the next biggest to this one' not of the relationships within the group as a whole, so that they had difficulty in inserting the second series which involved being aware of the possible positions in the whole series. They also had difficulty or failed to give the correct answer of the doll's position when the series was disarranged. Only the older children were able to complete all the requirements satisfactorily, understanding the stable relationships of number and length between the different steps and demonstrating this by the use of both cardinal and ordinal numbering. Piaget [41] gives this helpful summing-up of cardinal and ordinal numbering: 'A cardinal number is a class whose elements are conceived as "units" that are equivalent, and yet distinct in that they can be seriated, and therefore ordered. Conversely, each ordinal number is a series whose terms, though following one another according to the relations of order that determine their respective positions, are also units that are equivalent and can therefore be grouped as a class.'

A boy, six years three months, provides an example of seriation. He had been playing with the shop, became interested in the dates on the pennies, and spontaneously sorted them, writing down the following series:

1902	1908	1913	1915	1916	1919	1921
1927	1934	1936	1938	1939	1945	
1947	1962	1965	1966			

He could say what position each had in the series and also how many years there were between each penny.

The move from pre-operational to concrete operational thinking involves development from judgments based on percepts to those based on concepts. In this connection it is important to remember that, although the stage at which sensory-motor actions predominate ends at approximately two years of age, sensory-motor activity itself does not cease. The exploration of materials continues throughout the first school and beyond, and it is from these explorations that concepts are built. Mathematical concepts are constructed from the mathematical abstractions and generalizations which children make from their own actions on objects and situations. For example, it is the actions performed on many occasions of grouping and regrouping objects in a variety of ways that lead children to the understanding of conservation. The structuring of concepts also involves understanding of the relevance and irrelevance of specific attributes. For example, in the tests described earlier, children must appreciate that the spatial distribution of the eggs is irrelevant, as also is the height or width of vessels containing the liquid. Again, children developing concepts of shape must learn that colour or texture are irrelevant.

This brief consideration of concept development leads to some important implications in the development of children's mathematical thinking within the school environment. One of these is the need to provide throughout first school continuing opportunities to manipulate materials. The exploration of, for example, water, sand and clay is not completed in the reception class but is needed by seven-year-olds if they are to develop and elaborate concepts of conservation satisfactorily.

Secondly, accurate generalizations are more likely to be made as a result of experiences with a wide variety of materials and objects. A child's concept of seriation is likely to be more satisfactory if his understanding has arisen out of, and can be seen to be applicable to, many differing situations, for example, in sorting clothes and dolls in the home-corner, painting a picture of one's family, or, in scrap materials, making hangars to house a series of aeroplanes. There is a danger in thinking that mathematical concepts are learned more efficiently or only through special apparatus or materials. Such apparatus can be helpful, but the limiting and isolation of learning opportunities would seem to militate against good concept formation.

A wide range of materials and situations is also necessary in view of the personal nature of learning. Some children may develop concepts of reversibility primarily, for example, through extensive use of the water tray, others through the use of fabrics for sewing, while others may achieve it as a result of experiences in a variety of situations. It is emphasized throughout this book that real learning results from interaction with the environment, and mathematical understanding like all understanding is achieved by personal routes. Special apparatus and structured materials may help the learner to organize and codify this understanding, but do not provide fundamental meanings. For example, in learning about shape, the use of wooden templates alone would lead to inadequate concepts, but could help children to identify, codify and name shapes already observed and observable in flowers, furniture, buildings, etc.

The realization that in total experience the mathematical element is one among many only comes to a child as he discovers this to be so in different situations. In one seven-year-old class, 'birds' and 'snow' were two of a number of interests being pursued. Some children were painting pictures about birds or snow, others writing poems and stories and so on, but one child was interested in the hexagonal shape of snow crystals, and another group were measuring the height and length of different birds. In discussion and examination of each other's work the contribution of mathematics was recognized. It is through such individual and co-operative activity over a range of experiences that the place of mathematics in human experience is understood.

A teacher has a dual responsibility in the development of mathematical concepts, first in creating the basic environment within which the learning can take place, and second by intervening in children's learning, when appropriate, to help them focus on the relevant mathematical elements. Throughout this book the role of language in clarifying, refining and extending children's ideas is emphasized, and it is crucial in helping children to focus their thoughts on mathematical relationships.

In a reception class a four-year-old girl was playing with various pieces of scrap materials which included lids, boxes, bottles, etc. and three cylindrical shapes, viz: a small plastic cylinder, a metal tube of about the same size and a much larger cardboard roll. The teacher said to her: 'Can you put together the things you think go together?' The child then put together:

1. Lids
2. Boxes
3. Bottles
4. The two small cylinders.

The larger cardboard roll was not grouped with anything.

The teacher went through each group asking: 'Can you tell me why you put these together?' and when the two cylinders were reached the child replied: 'Because it's rolly.' Picking up the cardboard roll the teacher asked: 'Can this go anywhere?' and the child replied: 'Oh yes! It's rolly too!'

Thus as a result of questioning and thereby provoking the child to use language, a higher level of classification was reached, and this was achieved by the use of language which the child already possessed. On page 178 an example demonstrates the higher level of classification reached when the more precise terms 'animate' and 'inanimate' were given. It is possible in the present example that if the word 'cylinder' had been given to the child her focusing power would have increased further, for while the word 'rolly' is tied to actions which can be performed on objects, the word 'cylinder' refers to attributes of the objects themselves which can be applied to other similar objects on which such actions cannot be performed, for example, chimney pots, tree trunks, etc.

In another example the giving of the word 'pair' in relation to roller skates to a six-year-old girl caused her to differentiate between similar and symmetrical attributes, and as a result she drew up a list of 'pairs' including such things as socks, trousers, scissors, etc.

Discussion, question and comment provide opportunities for a teacher to give accurate language appropriate to the level of understanding reached by a child and can promote *further* thinking. At first school stage, precise language is particularly important in bringing about the move from perceptual to conceptual thought, for it is by language that abstracting and generalizing activity is brought into conscious awareness by a child and that the 'crystallization of relationships' is made possible.

However, the genuine use of language must not be confused with rote verbalism in which the words used are not the outcome of understanding. This can happen in mathematics where terms such as 'inches', 'pounds', 'sixpence', etc. can be learned and used by children without any understanding of what is meant. It is such spurious knowledge which can contribute towards later failure in mathematical development.

In first school it is not only through language that attention may be focused on mathematical attributes but also through the provision of appropriate equipment. For example, younger children may pay attention to the 'redness' of a bucket which makes the largest sand pie, and in such an instance the provision of an assortment of coloured buckets of the same size would encourage them to focus on the aspect of size. Similarly with older children the provision of balance scales could make it possible for them to refine their knowledge of units of weight.

The contribution of a teacher is therefore to provide both materials and language which are appropriate to the level of thinking reached by a child, but which also provoke the quest for further clarification and extension.

Specific concepts contribute towards the concept of number itself since they involve both classification and seriation as well as one-to-one correspondence. During first school, any activities which involve classification and seriation contribute towards a child's concept of number and possibilities for this occur in many classrooms. Number is both cardinal, i.e. 1, 2, 3, etc. (classification) and ordinal, i.e. 1st, 2nd, 3rd, etc. (seriation). Many examples can be commonly observed, for instance, in the home-corner, sorting clothes for children and dolls; comparing bed sizes, saucepans, plates, chairs; seriating bricks to make a staircase: selecting scrap materials to make beds for members of the family in a doll's house: seriating a collection of shells: making families of animals in clay. Frequent opportunities for one-to-one correspondence occur, for example, in putting one paint brush to one paint pot: distributing plates, knives etc. to individuals playing in the home-corner, aprons to children playing with sand or clay and instruments to children combining to make a band.

Such experiences form the basis of a concept of number; these then must be related to the number symbols. In cardinal form these have been, and are, encountered by children in many situations—out of school on buses, houses, telephones, trains, on many of their toys and in school on doors, boxes of crayons, in registers and so on. Children demonstrate their awareness of these by referring to them in speech or including them in drawings or paintings. Teachers can fit into and extend this knowledge by helping children to put known numbers in relation to those not known, thus building up an ordered sequence. It is important that number symbols should be learned alongside their meaning and not as a result of rote imitation. Apparatus is of limited value at this stage since it rarely matches the personal learning of a child, and is designed on the assumption that conservation has been achieved. An example of a five-year-old's drawn representation of peg-numbers he had just completed illustrates this:

This demonstrates the child's understanding of spatial 'surrounding' discussed earlier, but clearly this is confusing his concept of number.

As children reach conservation of number they show this in many and various ways. It is shown, for example, when a child 'counts on' at an appropriate time.

> Thirty-five bottles of milk were delivered to a class when forty-one were needed. When extra bottles were brought, the seven-year-old boy who had done the original counting said 'We need six more', and proceeded to count 'thirty-six, thirty-seven, . . .' as the bottles were added.

It may be shown as a child counts and groups collections on an interest table, or in a story. Children use written language to express mathematical ideas and the following example shows the level of conservation, seriation and reversibility reached by a six-year-old boy in relation to number and time—at least in relation to the days of the week:

> 'Eight more days said Bobby on Wednesday'
> 'Seven more days said Billy on Thursday'
> 'Six more days said Michael on Friday'
> 'Five more days said Lynne on Saturday'
> 'Four more days said Polly on Sunday'
> 'Three more days said Emily on Monday'

'Two more days said Jane on Tuesday'
'One more day said Carol on Wednesday'
'and it's today said Mother on Thursday'.
Thursday was the day their holiday began!

The achievement of conservation of number means that children can move on to the further stage of conceptualization of relationships between numbers. Such relationships include number sequence, number combinations, prime and non-prime numbers, place value and base, and relationships between numbers which produce number 'patterns', for example, odd and even numbers and tables.

It is important to emphasize that the ability to deal effectively with these numerical relationships is dependent on the development of mental structures within a child and not on the build-up of rote knowledge. Thus his understanding of twenty is the mental organization of many experiences of 'twenty-ness' which are conserved, and not on logical but imposed exercises of learning number combinations from one to ten and from eleven to twenty. There is still much to discover about the nature of children's mathematical development, but it seems clear that the size of a number does not necessarily cause difficulty in manipulation. Children (and some adults) find it easier to add 100 and 100 than 9 and 8, or again it is easier to add small to larger numbers than the reverse, thus $16 + 1$ may be easier than $3 + 7$. Except in simple practical situations, subtraction and division, which are reverse operations, are understood later than addition and multiplication which are cumulative.

Although cardinal and ordinal concepts appear to be interdependent, more attention is normally given to the former. It would seem important for children in first school to be given equal help in the formation of ordinal concepts both by drawing attention to the serial relationships in groups of objects and by giving the necessary language. Many stories for children involve first, second and third positions, but few go beyond this— 'The Twelve Dancing Princesses' is an exception—and children may easily be inhibited in the development of ordination unless the further vocabulary of fourth, fifth, etc. is given. The following story illustrates how ordinal development breaks down after the third choice:

My best shop is the Toy shop. If I had enough money I would buy the biggest teddy because I only have a few. My second choice would be a sewing set. I do not think I would show it to my Grandpa because he would ask me to darn his socks. My third choice would be a doll. Actually I would like a doll's house with real curtains. Because my one's hinges come off and the door is loose. I might buy one of those trolls with long hair.

Apparatus and structured material may be helpful in the development of number concepts, for example, the abacus or the hundred board. Whatever apparatus is used it should help children to order their own mathematical ideas, i.e. they should be able to use it in a variety of ways suitable to their ideas and interests, and not only in a predetermined manner. For example, the following is a list of ways in which a group of seven-year-old children used a hundred board:

1. Put on discs horizontally from left to right.
2. Put on discs horizontally from right to left.
3. Put on discs vertically from top to bottom.
4. Took out alternate discs leaving even numbers.
5. Took out alternate discs leaving odd numbers.
6. Made table patterns, e.g.   3   6   9
                                 12   15   18
                              21   24   27
7. Made a 'magic square' by putting on all the discs, except one, in a random arrangement, then moving them one at a time until the correct numerical order was achieved.

A hundred board can be used in a rigid, and therefore limited manner, or creatively as in this example, as a base from which children can discover numerical relationships up to 1,000 or further.

All mathematical thinking involves relationships. At the simplest level, the concept of one-to-one correspondence deals with a simple relationship between the individual members of two groups, while at the next level the concept of number includes at the same time the relationships of classification and seriation. The development of mathematical thinking involves the understanding of increasingly complex relationships, and it is important that when children have reached the stage of conservation of number they should proceed to more complex relationships as discussed above.

This principle of helping children to understand increasingly complex relationships applies to all areas of mathematical knowledge. The simple identification of aspects of the world according to shape, and the grouping of objects on the criterion of common shape involves simple relationships, i.e. that triangularity, for example, is defined by three-sidedness, and possessing an acute angle is not a satisfactory criterion. However, once children are able to recognize and group objects according to shape, they should go on to perceive more complex relationships, for example, symmetry and tessellation (the discovery of which regular figures can be fitted together exactly, for example, rectangles and hexagons, and which cannot, for example, octagons). The following is an example of a teacher leading a child toward further relational thinking, and also illustrates her good use of the environment to further the child's learning.

> A vertically grouped class of children had been interested in shape, and a seven-year-old boy was scrutinizing a cylindrical magnet closely:
> Teacher: 'What shape is it?'
> Boy: 'It's a round oblong'.
> The teacher took the magnet and, demonstrating by holding it towards him so that it could be seen from the appropriate perspectives, said:
>> 'Yes. It's round if you look at it this way, and oblong if you look at it this way'.
> She gave the boy the words 'circle' and 'rectangle', and then suggested that he looked at other three-dimensional objects in the room from different perspectives to see what he could discover. This led him to the knowledge that while the sphere looks spherical from all perspectives, other three-dimensional shapes do not.

With six-year-old children also interested in shapes, including circles, another teacher encouraged relational thinking in general by asking the children to try to think why bottle necks and corks are circular rather than any other shape.

Reference was made earlier to symmetry as an aspect of more complex relationships involved in developing spatial concepts. The following example illustrates the understanding of symmetrical relationships of a boy of six-and-a-half years.

> He brought the drawing (to which letters have been added for clarification) to his teacher with the comment:
> 'Half of this is symmetrical.'

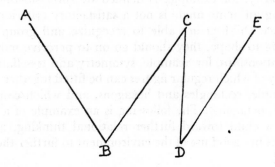

> Asked what he meant he replied:
> 'Well, that half (AB/CB) is symmetrical, but that half (CD/ED) is not symmetrical, only half of it is. That (AB) is symmetrical to that (CB) but that (CD) is not symmetrical to that (ED). But if you look carefully, that (AB) is symmetrical to that (CB) and is also symmetrical to that (ED). So the only line which is not symmetrical is that (CD). So that (CB) is symmetrical to that (ED), and that (CD) is the odd one out.'

This example shows very clearly the mobility of thought characteristic of concrete operational thinking discussed earlier.

Just as the concept of conservation is basic to a functional use of numbers so also must it underlie the use of any standard unit of measurement, i.e. of length, weight, time or money. Children can 'do sums' by means of rote learning without understanding the concept of number, so also can they manipulate scales, a ruler or a clock. This is sometimes seen when they learn to tell the time at the hour or half-past, but are completely nonplussed by quarter-to and past. The facility for perceptual learning demonstrated by children in first school can easily lead to rote learning and be misinterpreted as conceptual understanding, so that it is important to differentiate between them.

The concept of length is usually developed before that of weight or time. The subjective element in time, for example that it seems to vary in duration depending on the degree of personal involvement in an activity, and also that it cannot be seen and handled, may help to explain its difficulty. Similarly, if an object is too heavy for a young child to push or lift it remains static and its weight cannot be experienced through a child's own actions. An example of this occurred when a group of seven-year-olds who had been discussing the weight of various objects were asked how much they thought the block of flats visible from their room might weigh.

> The children looked surprised, and one said, 'Those don't weigh anything.' When asked to explain he replied, 'Well, you couldn't put *those* on the scales!'

However, children do experience extensive length in, for example, walking along streets, helping to put sheets on a bed, having a long piece of string on a toy and so on.

Most five-year-olds are still unable to conserve length. When they cut off a piece of thread, for instance, it may be two inches or two feet in length, bearing no relation to the length of seam to be sewn. Legs on a stool made at the woodwork bench are likely to be four in number but each of a different length.

The introduction of standard units of inches, feet or yards to children at this level of understanding inevitably leads to inaccurate use and conclusions.

> A five-year-old used a yard ruler to measure a table four feet long. She placed the ruler to one end of the table, discovered that it did not reach to the further side and so slid it along until it matched. Then she counted the inches, missing out some in the process, and concluded that the table measured twenty-nine inches. In another class a group of boys had been building high towers with bricks and the teacher introduced a yard ruler thinking that they would be interested to find out how high the towers were. It was greeted with enthusiasm by one boy, although he refused to measure the towers or other objects of appropriate length, but instead tried to measure

the length of the home-corner and classroom, getting hope-
lessly confused in the process. Other children did not even
relate it to measuring at all, but used it as a gun, a spear and as
the stick of a jumping-stand.

In developing concepts of length, capacity, etc. understanding in terms of intensive aspects precedes that of extensive
aspects: long/short, heavy/light comes before 'longest' as
measured, 'lightest' as weighed and so on. The concept of
length is achieved through many situations of matching and
comparing lengths, for example, in sewing, model-making
and woodwork, and in comparing heights with other children,
or their own height compared with the top of a cupboard, etc.
It is through such experiences that ideas of 'longer than',
'shorter than' develop which indicates the beginning of understanding of conservation since it implies a stable relationship
between the two items being compared. An example of this
from a five-year-old class occurred after the children had heard
a story about a giant.

> They were asking how tall he would be, whether he would be as
> big as the door or bigger. One boy said:
> 'He would be bigger than that. I should think that a giant's
> boys and girls as old as us would be as big as you, Miss X,
> and we would be as big as a giant's baby.'

Once children have conserved length they can be encouraged
to apply and use this understanding in many appropriate
situations, to measure a doll before making a dress, to decide
how long the legs of a stool should be and so on. In one class
of seven-year-olds where there was a collection of sycamore
seeds, some children had been blowing them to see how they
were dispersed by the wind and found that they could blow
them varying distances. This led to the making of a comparative
list and the discovery that the shortest distance blown was $7\frac{1}{2}$
inches and the furthest 5 feet 10 inches.

At this stage children need a wide variety of measuring
instruments to experiment with and to discover increasing relationships in linear measurement and its relations to other mathematical concepts, for example, to time leading to speed. Inch
tapes, surveyors' wheels and tapes make it possible to measure
circular objects or longer distance.

A measuring rope enabled a seven-year-old to discover the answer to a question which had arisen in a class discussion about giraffes:

'Just now I measured how high the classroom was and it was 15 feet high from the ground to the ceiling. A giraffe is 20 feet high so a giraffe couldn't get in our classroom at all. So the classroom will have to be 5 more feet and so then a giraffe could get in our classroom after all. He can also run as fast as a car and he can go 30 miles an hour. So he could go 60 miles only he would do it in 2 hours instead.'

It is important to utilize the variety of experiences children have concerned with length. Many travel long journeys by car and are interested in distances between towns and times taken. (The example on page 93 illustrates this.) Another group of seven-year-olds were interested in the comparative distances they would travel on their summer holidays, and became very involved in discussing these. It is easy in a classroom to become limited to experiences with smaller units of measurement: inches/feet, minutes/hours, ounces/pounds, etc. Children should be encouraged to draw on their experiences of larger units, for example miles, months/years, stones/tons, and be given opportunities in school to pay attention to these when possible, for example, to record how long plants take to grow, to note their own weight when medically examined or to record the delivery of coke or potatoes. It is the thinking which develops out of observations and discussions of such situations which leads to the awareness and understanding of the increasingly complex relationships referred to earlier.

The development of concepts of capacity and weight are dependent on the achievement of conservation in liquid quantity and substance, with weight developing slightly the later so that this is more likely to become established during the junior school. Because of this, children in first school need many opportunities for experience with substances, for example, clay, wet sand and cooking ingredients, in order to develop the concept. Similarly experimenting at the water trolley, dispensing milk in the home-corner, and filling paint-pots and flower vases are the kind of experiences which will lead to this understanding in relation to liquids. Once this stage is reached, the provision of apparatus is necessary to extend knowledge, to test out assumptions and to find solutions.

Simple balance scales and pint/quart containers are inadequate and need to be supplemented by, for example, spring balance, letter and bathroom scales, and gills, gallons and cooking measures. Accuracy of measurement is now possible and important in children's experimenting, and should be encouraged both by providing precision equipment and opportunities for cooking more complicated recipes etc. In one seven-year-old class the birth of a family of guinea-pigs led to progressive and accurate records being kept of their weight and length in relation to age. This experience was only possible because they had access to proper equipment which enabled them to work out quite complex mathematical relationships.

The children in this example had an established concept of time involving weeks and days of the week but when most children first come to school their ideas of time are unstable. In their own homes they will have learned the sequence of events which make up a day, but coming to school introduces an entirely new pattern. They are often confused while this is being learned and have difficulty in differentiating between morning and afternoon, play-time and dinner-time. No wonder the statement, 'Mummy will come for you at 12 o'clock' sometimes fails to comfort. Much of the distress experienced by children when starting school is caused by the limitations of pre-operational thought in which the lack of spatial, temporal, object conservation makes it impossible for a child to conceive that while he is engaged in various activities in school, his home still exists where mother is working and to which he will return when lunch-time comes. A teacher of young children has to help them to sort out the sequence of events in school connected at appropriate points to time as recorded on a clock, and enable them gradually to relate these to out of school events: breakfast-time, tea-time, weekends, etc. Slowly the organization of events becomes extended and stabilized. These centre on a child's own life and experiences and at first, therefore, appropriately extend into exploration of time past rather than future. Children can usefully be encouraged to bring photographs of themselves as babies, or on holiday the previous year. Following this, a six-year-old wrote a book entitled 'Things that are older

than me'. The first page read, 'I am six years old and everything in this book is older than that.' Other contributions were
of her sister 'nine years old', her mummy 'older than me',
and the school 'about four years older than me'.

Any cumulative pictorial or verbal records of events within
a school help children to develop concepts of temporal continuity, for example, the gradual development of tadpoles into
frogs, of chicks into pullets or of horse-chestnut buds opening.
These encourage children to think back over days and weeks
and to relate the events recorded to other situations which
occurred at those times.

As a concept of time is established, the recording of the
passing of time on clock and calendar can be understood, and
it is at this stage that children need a variety of different
calendars and timing devices to help them to elaborate and
refine this knowledge. For example:

> Two seven-year-olds were sailing small boats in a water-tray,
> and were speculating on whose would reach the other side
> first. The teacher suggested timing the boats and introduced
> a stop watch. Subsequently the children investigated and
> recorded various activities which could be completed in a
> certain time. These included:
>
> > 'In one second I can put my hand up.'
> > 'It took Alan 2 seconds to bang 6 times on the drum.'
> > 'It took Susan 5 seconds to press all the numbers down on
> > the till.'
> > 'It took John 6 minutes to serve a customer.'

This interest in timing was extended to the general routine
in the classroom and, amongst others, records were kept of
how long it took to clear up each day with, to the teacher, a
welcome speeding up of the process as they tried to beat the
previous day's time! Other timing devices which can be helpful
are alarm clocks, egg-timers and cooking timers, while candle
and water clocks often lead children to experiment in making
their own clocks, for example, dry sand pouring through a
hole in a yoghurt container.

By the end of first school some children will have developed time concepts ranging from an interest in historical time,
for example, the development of ships from a hollowed out log

to diesel oil, to the accurate organization of time, hours, minutes and seconds using the twenty-four hour clock as, for example, in making a time-table in connection with a train interest. This example shows how far a concept as complex as time can develop during the first school period.

The development of the concept of area is even more difficult because this is dependent on an understanding of euclidian relationships which is not reached by most children until the end of junior school. During first school topological notions of objects in space are dominant, for example, enclosure, proximity etc. but the notion of space itself is not yet present. A familiar situation in a reception class is of a large box or piece of fabric from the centre of which a child has cut a tiny piece—thus ruining it for a larger piece of work! When searching for a piece of cardboard or material, children at this stage will often discard any from which a piece has been cut, although more than enough remains for their requirement. These situations illustrate children's lack of awareness of a piece as a whole unit capable of division into a number of smaller units.

By the end of first school, most children can use such material more effectively: this is still on the level of practical intelligence —of perceiving relationships between the size and shape of the required items, for example, car wheels, and the actual material available. An interest in, and ability to identify euclidian shapes such as rectangles, triangles etc. is often found amongst young children, but it must be remembered that their attention is on perceptual features such as sidedness and points, and not on the relationship between those features and the space enclosed. Many opportunities can be found in a classroom for experience in paying attention to this aspect which is fundamental to later conceptual understanding, and reference has already been made to children's experimentation with shape. A teacher needs to help children to learn how to use cardboard etc. efficiently, and therefore economically, how to fit bricks into a box, which shapes of plastic will cover a table and so on, and further, to help them by verbalizing in statement or discussion to abstract the critical features which led to the final arrangement.

Learning about money is considered last because the present situation will be changed by the introduction of decimal currency and this could cause problems for teachers of young children. However, this is only likely to happen where children are submitted to a mechanical approach to the present currency, unrelated to their level of understanding and experience of money outside school. Children will be involved with adults as new coins are introduced and packaging and labelling are changed, and it would seem that what is necessary is for teachers to keep pace with the children's experience and questions concerning the new system, and not to initiate specific teaching. As the time for the change-over approaches, interest and attention will be directed to the new currency, and it is likely that many children at the end of first school will be able to adapt to the new system without difficulty. This is because at this stage they understand a money system to be made up of stable value relationships between the various coins. In decimal currency the relationships will be more simple, but these will be understood in so far as a child has reached concrete operational thought. If he knows that one sixpence is equal in value to six pennies although the latter appears to be more, he will also understand that a 'five' is equal in value to five new pennies.

It is to be hoped that children will learn about the new currency by actually handling the new coins and not cardboard or plastic imitations. The satisfactory development of concepts is based on sensory-motor and mental actions performed in relevant contexts. Children learn to tell the time by observation and reference to accurate working clocks and other time-devices; weight is understood as a result of weighing real materials on proper scales. It is by the presence of such equipment and its appropriate use by both teacher and children that increasing complexity in interaction between percept and concept can develop.

One of the ways in which children test out and check their conclusions is by appropriate recording, and many of the examples included have illustrated this. However, recording itself does not teach children, but, first, is a means enabling them to organize or reorganize what they already know, and it may be an individual or co-operative enterprise:

> A girl of nearly eight years made 'A history book about myself' in which she gave a selection of details and illustrations of

herself from two to seven years of age. In another class a group
of seven-year-olds had contributed towards a book 'About
Numbers'. The page on '2' included:

'two, second, pair, couple, double, twin, bicycle, duet, dual,
2 o'clock.'

Secondly, recording enables children to order knowledge
so that comparisons and relationships can be discovered:
for example, graphs can crystallize for comparison a set of
observations, either where the number of items is too great
to be scrutinized without recording, for example, the makes
of cars owned by parents, or where the mathematical observations apply over a time span, for example, the growth of plants
or animals. The comparison of times described on page 109
could only be achieved by referring to the entries made daily
into a book.

Further, recording may be used by a child to gain further
knowledge, or may itself lead to the discovery of new facts.

A seven-year-old boy said to his teacher:

'My birthday was on Tuesday last year but it's going to be
on Wednesday this year. Can I make a list of all people's
birthdays (i.e. all in his class) and see what day their birthdays are on?'

In a six-year-old class, a girl who had decided to write out
the numbers from one to a hundred on a squared blackboard
suddenly exclaimed,

'Look! All the ones are under each other, and all the
twos . . .', and continued up to the tens.

Children must themselves understand the purpose of any
recording they undertake and this may range from the boy
who wrote down the number facts he had discovered at the
water-tray so that he could tell his mother, to the seven-year-
old who wanted to discover how many different ways there were
to make twenty. Purposefulness of this quality is not present in
the rote reproduction of, for example, number bonds or clock
faces. This is often a perseverating activity undertaken at adult
request involving a child in the reproduction of known material
which has long since ceased to be of interest to him.

A child's purpose in recording is often to assimilate new understanding. A six-year-old girl who had just discovered how to 'add one' produced a whole page of additions, and the example on page 98 shows how a child was assimilating the idea of a pair. The contribution of practice to children's learning is discussed again in Chapter 10, but it is important to refer to it in this chapter since it often appears to be thought that practice *per se* is a major element in the development of mathematics. This is so only when it is a self-initiated assimilatory activity.

Practice of this kind often leads to further accommodation. The child described, who practised the addition of one, showed these to her teacher who asked her if she could add numbers *to* one. She went away and thought for a while then solved the problem and produced a selection of such additions. The teacher's contribution here, and in other examples included in this chapter, draws attention to the role of problems in the development of mathematical ideas. The earlier discussion on relational thinking is also relevant here, since problems are concerned with generalizing a specific mathematical idea to other appropriate situations, i.e. relational thinking. The examples of the teacher's questions on page 103 illustrate the development of relational thinking through problems raised by the teacher but many other problems are posed by children themselves as a result of their own activity. The common principle in these situations is the relevance of the problem to a child's own exploration into mathematical ideas arising out of a personal interest or activity. In this connection, frequent opportunities arise for estimating amounts or quantities: 'How much butter do you think we have?' 'How many sheets do you think you can cut from that material?' and so on. Examining the result against the original estimate encourages the perceptual and conceptual refining discussed earlier.

The methods used in solving problems will vary from child to child, being dependent both on experiences and levels of thinking. A teacher can encourage children to attempt various methods in the solution of problems in order to discover which is the most efficient and economical, i.e. which is the most elegant method. Elegance is an important mathematical criterion, and whilst children in first school are too young to consider this, they can be helped to discover a personally satisfying method of solution. For example, a group of seven-year-olds correctly answered that $9+7=16$. When their teacher asked them how they had worked this out, one had added $9+1$, $9+2$, etc., another knew that $9+9=18$ and had then subtracted one and one, and a third knew that $10+7=17$ so had subtracted one, i.e. the most economical and efficient method. On another occasion a child decided to use a measuring rope to measure a corridor in preference to a number of foot rulers.

The main function of the first school in relation to mathematical development, is to provide children with the environment and help which will enable them to begin to bring about a match between the personal psychological learning structures which they have been developing since birth, and the logical structures of mathematical knowledge. In this Chapter mathematics has been seen as a part of a child's total intellectual development. Nathan Isaacs [23] emphasized that this intrinsic unity should:

> be *preserved* and not *severed* by our educational approach. . . . It is only preserved in so far as, first of all, children start forming their own true inward structured idea of number; and secondly, if the later rule-learning, operation-learning and so on, becomes a living graft on that idea, or rather, is successfully developed as a further stage of its own inward growth.

CHAPTER 7

Music: Hearing and Making Sound

THE BABY'S cries are the first expression of himself in sound: the kicking of his arms and legs brings his limbs into contact with the things about him and he builds a pattern of banging activity, unwittingly causing sound. Together with the sucking reflex these make the ready-made behaviour patterns with which he is born and which he exercises in his first month. There is some evidence of pre-natal vocalizing and there is no doubt about the kicking! We also know that there is a physiological response to sound in pulse and breathing even on the first day, and some evidence of electrical activity of the brain in response to sound before birth. The baby is born into a world of sound, much of which will not be music to adult ears. Consequently the musical content of such sound and its relevance to the development of aural perception is often overlooked. When he is born, response to sound is shown by changes in facial expression and a cessation of crying. His organization of this and other sense and motor modes will establish the foundation of his later responses to his environment.

In the first weeks of life the sound of his mother's voice will occur in his presence more often than any other sound. Because of the relationship a mother has with her new baby, the tone of voice will be consistent, soft, soothing, flowing smoothly (legato), rather than crisp and short sounding (staccato). The gentle, sometimes barely perceptible, rocking of a mother cradling her baby imbues her talking or vocalizing with its rhythm. The baby becomes familiar with the sound of her and his recognition of her is accompanied by pleasure. A baby of three months turned his head at the sound of his mother's voice. Later her sound became something to look for and this action pattern was extended as he began to look for other sounds which had become familiar through their repetition. At nine months he looked for the telephone when it rang, having recognized its sound. The sound of his mother using different tones of voice in the same way became familiar to him, extending his recognitive response. Most people's voices are expressive of their mood and meaning and of their relationship with the person to whom they are talking. An angry voice is often louder and uses a higher pitch range than usual, indeed we talk of 'raised voices'. Most voices have a pleasing rise and fall of pitch. We tend to notice the absence of this rather than its presence, finding it difficult to listen to a monotonous (literally, on one note) voice. Experience of a wider range of pitch and tone quality (timbre) will result from recognition of father's voice.

A pitch slide (glissando) that ascends occurs when some machines are switched on, e.g. vacuum cleaners, washing machines, spin-driers, mixers: when switched off they produce a descending pitch slide. A whistling kettle produces similar glissandos at a much higher pitch. Some vacuum cleaners, hair-driers and car-horns produce two notes in pitch simultaneously, very often a third apart, and many police cars, ambulances, fire engines and trains produce two notes in pitch successively, the interval varying between a second, third and fourth. Successive pitch changes are caused by the filling of vessels: saucepans, buckets, kettles, baths, etc. In our world things continually come and go: aeroplanes fly overhead, cars and trains pass, footsteps approach and depart. As they come nearer their sound becomes louder (crescendo) and as they go further away the sound dies away (diminuendo). Sounds begin either with the sudden impact of the very loud (fortissimo) or they gradually get going (accelerando); they stop either suddenly or by gradually slowing down (rallantando) In sleeping, walking, sucking, breathing, in the child's own heartbeat, his mother's heartbeat and in his digestive functioning, patterns of rhythm and order are first experienced. Later the child becomes familiar with everyday household noises which have a rhythmic content: an even tread upstairs or along the passage, walking or running, the brushing of a carpet, the door-knocker, egg-beating, ticking and striking of clocks, chopping, hammering, raking, coffee percolating and the telephone bell. And of course there will be music to a greater or lesser extent in every household. In some homes pop music may be playing for most of the day: others may have little music of any sort other than the signature tunes and background music for T.V. programmes. Luckily most children are sung or crooned or chanted to when they are babies, if not when they are toddlers.

Vocal sound is a basic mode of human expression and at first it often expresses discomfort as the baby is usually asleep when he is contented. His cries begin to form a pattern, the degree of discomfort extending the pitch range. When he begins to cheep and gurgle contentedly his tone of voice is different. It soon becomes obvious when the baby's sounds are communicative or when they are expressive of mood or experimental, for he begins to imitate the sounds he makes himself, repeating them over and over again and finding great satisfaction in this activity. This repetition indicates a rudimentary analysis of sound. Inevitably the sounds children make will be affected by the richness of sounds in their environment.

> A boy (five months) accurately produced intervals of a fourth and fifth from the same starting note. His sound environment was particularly rich, his parents regularly practising instrumental and vocal music; this obviously encouraged his accommodative activity.

Children's experience of reproducing their own sounds accurately helps them to accommodate to external stimuli with more and more success: they make progressive approximations of the sounds they try to imitate.

A girl (1.0) sang this:

The adult with her imitated the sound; the little girl smiled and joined in. The adult then pitched the sound a 4th higher. After several attempts to imitate the new  pitch, it was momentarily achieved, lost and found again, much to the child's delight.

This exemplifies the role of adults in fostering the development of aural perception in young children by observing and imitating the sounds the children themselves make and providing models for imitation which are a slight extension of these sounds. An analysis in terms of the musical grammar is helpful but not essential: sounds can be made higher or lower by a little or a lot: they can be made softer or louder, longer or shorter: they can be made with a different vowel or consonant and they can be made singly or in groups.

In the first few weeks the baby's motor activity brings his limbs into contact with the things near him, for example his legs bang against the side of the cot (see Chapter 5). His movements are often accompanied by vocalizing. As his hand and eye movements become co-ordinated he learns to take hold of objects. Once the object is held the motor activity sometimes continues with the object still in the hand. If the child is in his pram the object coming into contact with the covers will make a dull thud, but if he is on the floor the sound will be more distinct.

> A boy (8 months) grasped the soft toy in his pram and banged the cover with it making a slight noise. On another occasion a wooden brick was grasped and banged against the floor making a louder noise.

From this activity the intention of producing sounds by banging on the floor develops, and the child is using an instrument. Objects which have previously been for sucking and grasping are now also for banging with. We can foster this development by considering not only the shape, size, colour and safety of the objects available for the baby, but also their sound possibilities. During his second and third years the child's behaviour patterns become more mobile as memory develops and allows for *delayed* imitation.

> A girl (1.6) witnessed another little girl's temper tantrum and was very interested in the spectacle. Several days later when she was crying angrily she suddenly altered the sound of her crying in imitation of the other child's sound.
>
> A boy (3.2) enjoyed a television programme about a lion very much. A very convincing roar was *playfully* used in mock

attack. The sound and the movements were serious, but the facial expression teasing.

When children go to school for the first time it is likely that their mode of musical functioning will vary according to the age of entry. We would expect a reception class of five-year-olds to have reached a further stage of development than a nursery class of three-year-olds. We also know that earlier environmental opportunity contributes to these differences. Whenever he comes to school the child comes as a developing being: his earliest years have furnished evidence beyond doubt of the capacity for development of the human organism (see introduction). Then school intervenes. What are the criteria by which we judge such intervention? We know that the quality of learning is affected by environmental opportunity. This holds good whatever stage the child is at, for it is the actions he brings to bear on his environment that constitute his learning and, indeed, which constitute his experience. If we are concerned that children's learning should help them to understand our cultural discipline of music, we must take account of musical criteria in planning the school environment (see Chapter 3). A child's early development of vocalizing and of causing sound by banging helps us to see how.

When a teacher meets a new group of children she has to find some common ground, some shared experience which can serve as a starting point for their activities together. As it is likely that many of the group will have sung the same nursery rhymes, singing provides an immediate common ground. The ability to reproduce pitch patterns accurately (to sing a tune accurately but at your own pitch) and to accommodate to specific pitch (to sing in tune at somebody else's given pitch) develops at different rates in individual children. Children have to *learn* to sing in tune, making successive approximations of a melody line until the whole song falls into place, exactly in the same way as babies learn to imitate their own and other people's sounds. It is a step further in their development to be able to sing a song at a given pitch.

A boy (3) sang 'Baa baa black sheep' almost accurately at his own pitch. At 2.6 the beginning interval (5th) and the last note only were in place. A girl (6) was rarely in tune when she began to sing; a tuning-in period was necessary during which her singing became more accurate. Sometimes she could sing in tune with the adult, but at other times she could not. Songs she had known for some time fell into place more easily than new ones. The need for repetition was implicit in her behaviour.

When singing songs to themselves or with a group of friends young children intuitively pitch the songs in their developed ranges of voice. This is based on their range of speaking voice and is lower in pitch than is suggested by the keys in which songs are written in songbooks for young children. A survey carried out by Charles Cleall (Novello Primer 134) gave the following results:

		A_1	A	D^1
Infant	Boys	54%	56%	28%
	Girls	68%	44%	25%

This chart indicates the percentage of infant children who could sing A below middle C (A_1), A above middle C (A), and top D —the second D above middle C (D^1). The range of voice develops gradually with much experience of vocalizing and singing and this development is hindered, indeed in some cases prevented, if songs are continually presented to children in a pitch range to which they cannot accommodate. Furthermore, however simple the accompaniment, constant accompanied singing prevents children's perception of their out-of-tuneness, thus hindering the development of accuracy in the reproduction of pitch. Unaccompanied singing in an appropriate key is essential for this development. At times, of course, if the teacher is able, songs can be accompanied on keyboard, guitar, or with any of the instruments in the room giving the children opportunity to sing with an accompaniment and thus extending their musical experience. Singing a song to children, just as telling a story or reading a poem, involves the teacher's communication of an idea to them and involves the children in a group response which contributes to their social awareness and development. It seems much more appropriate to sit

Plate 32 (also *33*)   Challenges allowing individual response from the children.

Plate 33

Plate 34 Fine touch and sustainment.

Plate 35 The attitude of the body may be a contributory factor in the expression of mood.

Plate 36

Plate 37

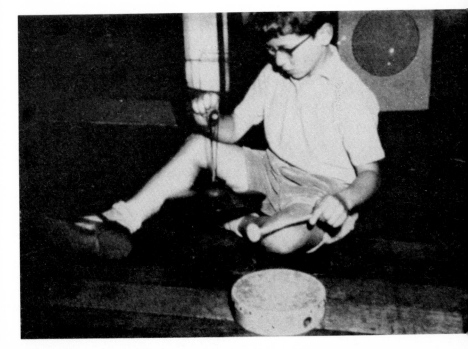

Plate 38

Plate 39

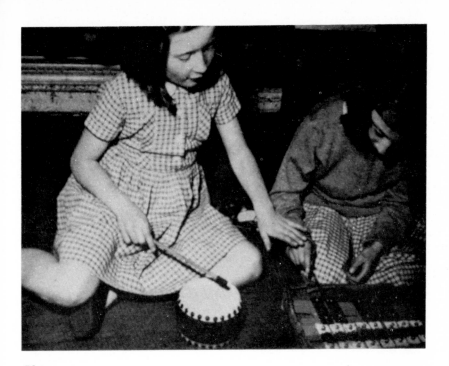

Plate 40

Plate 41

Plate 42

Plate 43

Plate 44

Plate 45

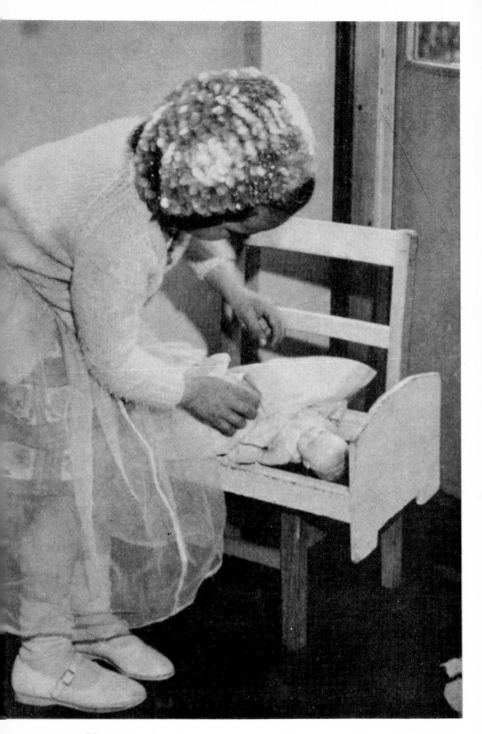

Plate 46

Plate 47

Plate 48

Plate 49

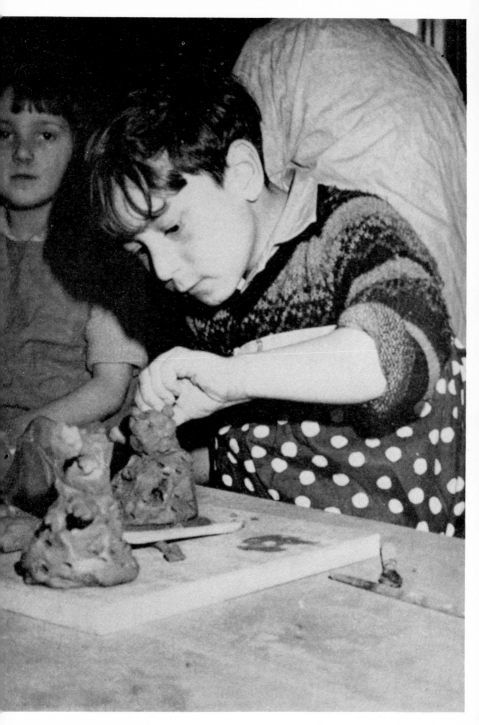

Plate 50

Plate 51

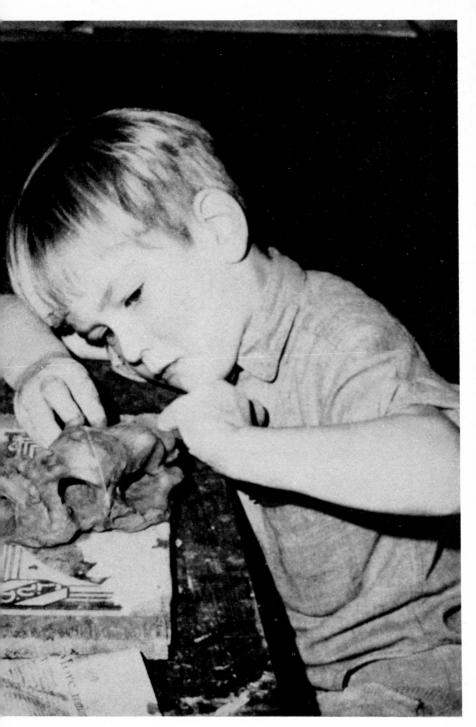

Plate 52

informally with children for singing as usually happens for story telling, for the ease and relaxation of the situation enables them to focus on the particular problems involved. If the classroom is accoustically difficult, and many old ones are, the group may need to sit close together if the teacher is to be heard without forcing her own singing tone. If teachers are not confident of their singing ability an instrument can help them. An alto xylophone (notes named for poor readers of notation) or an alto melodica (blown evenly and gently) are of appropriate pitch for young children's singing and enable the teacher still to be part of the group while playing them.

We plan our intervention in order to *foster* development. Children's early vocalizing builds the foundation for later singing activity and helps them to learn about their own vocal possibilities. Children often vocalize as they are moving, indeed it seems as if moving and sounding are part of one experience for young children (see Chapter 5).

During one outside playtime for nursery and infant children these pieces of vocalizing were heard:

long-lasting shouted calls of children's names:
two children running across the playground making sounds in time with their running:

six children in a partially enclosed area running round and round trying only to step on some wooden shapes lying scattered on the ground; their sounds expressed their excitement at the task they had set themselves and when collision threatened they produced consistently high pitched descending glissandi:

a girl walking across the playground sang:

whilst travelling, a group of girls chanted to this rhythm:

a boy sang out: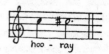

a boy doing up his coat buttons with some difficulty sang to himself; his sound reflected his calm and was as confident and unhurried as his movements. He knew it could be achieved in the end.

The appropriateness of the teacher's intervention is a matter for her present judgment. Many times, outside and inside, invaluable opportunities such as these will arise, when it is possible to draw children's attention to their own sounds and to sounds happening in the environment or made by other children, to suggest that they might join in, or imitate or describe the sounds and to discuss the cause of the sound or the reason for its special quality. These questions and comments and efforts to reproduce sounds lay the foundation for the music student's aural training classes. But there is a difference: the demands on the music student are external and from the point of view of the discipline of music; they are concerned with his professional equipment as a musician. The teacher's demands, on the other hand, are made from the point of view of the individual child's development. A child's activity indicates his stage of development; the activities of a group of children give similar indications.

A group of six-year-olds were having a discussion about sounds.

Teacher: Will you try to copy *my* sounds exactly. Listen very carefully.
Boy: And watch!
Teacher: Why do you say that?
Boy: Because of the shape of your mouth.
Girl: I'll keep an eye *and* an ear on you!

The sounds they were asked to reproduce were selected from sounds they had made on the previous day as part of some movement work. The teacher also extended the sounds in order to find out which children could accommodate to the new element, a glissando covering a wider range of pitch, ascending instead of descending, soft instead of loud. In this way the teacher is able to assess the development of each child and of the group. As the pitch range is extended songs can be pitched in a higher key. The group of six-year-olds mentioned above were very fond of the song 'Farmer Higgs' (O.U.P. School Music Book). Recognition of the first phrase—not yet sung in its written key of G—developed very quickly and it was remarked on even when occurring in the middle of a tune or with a different rhythm scheme. The teacher asked them to sing the phrase:

beginning first on middle C then on D and E and so on. Singing a phrase at successively higher or lower pitches in this manner constitutes a sequence. At the end of this sequence when the phrase was begun on G many children had lost the pitch although they had all been accurate beginning on C, D and E. With this in mind the teacher then asked for the phrase to be copied beginning on E. This time many children could not do this accurately: the effect of being off pitch lasted over to the E pitch.

The importance of the role of the teacher in intervening *appropriately*, i.e. in pitch, cannot be overemphasized. The last part of the example suggests that the approach to a problem is critical, and specifically that in their next discussion those children would need to approach the E pitch from one in which they had been successful.

> In a similar situation this question was posed to a group of seven-year-olds in a more technical manner, their vocabulary of words relevant to musical activity having developed during the year.

Teacher: Let's test your pitch range.
Can you produce these sounds accurately?

All the children were successful in a range of eight notes (an octave) from the A below middle C to the A above middle C (A$_1$–A), but after A the accuracy began to deteriorate as the children attempted to sing the higher notes. There was great amusement at the mixture of sounds produced in the effort to accommodate to the higher pitch, and many children began to practise singing up to high notes. In the next discussion some progress was evident. At the suggestion of one of the children this exercise was later extended to a song. It was sung in the scales (key) A, B, C, D, etc. and later still in high A, B, etc.

The group were aware that they were stretching their pitch range. A point of musical grammar which had clearly been assimilated was the idea of key, though it was not yet known by the correct term. The children knew that songs could be sung at different pitches using the notes of particular scales. This group were aware of their own development and of each other's. They were beginning to see how they could help themselves, by practising high notes, for example, bringing a problem-solving attitude to aural activity. Any of them learning an instrument later would already have ideas about practising and would be able to make their practice productive. All too often practice becomes a rote repetitiveness because children have no real understanding of its purposes or of the musical ideas involved (see Chapter 10).

A group of eight-year-olds were slower in their pitch development than the group of younger children mentioned above. Many of them were children with emotional difficulties, whose rate of intellectual development was consequently slowed down. This was reflected in their musical activity. To help them it was necessary for the teacher to extend their vocalizing experience in as many ways as possible so that they could learn about their own vocal possibilities. Making up games and stories and working with movement all helped this awareness to grow. There was great satisfaction when it became apparent that their pitch was becoming more accurate: the songs sounded better! A class of six-year-olds were fascinated by a recording of the bells at the abbey at Beuron which had been chosen by older children for assembly. The vibrating of the different sizes of bells and the cacophony of overtones impressed

the children who later experimented themselves to produce
lasting vibrations. Many of them decided that 'ding' and
'dong' sounds finishing with closed teeth provided the most
effective vocal way. Pairs of children decided to sing different
notes and from this grew the idea of pitching a note and
holding it steadily, not moving off it even a fraction, while
someone else came in on another note. This very simple mode
of producing harmonic texture developed their perception of
aural space. The children extended the activity. Three or four
notes were pitched one after the other and held and the
demands made on the last voice to enter became specific:
'Pitch a note lower than the lowest.' 'Pitch it where there is a
large gap'. 'Pitch it just below the highest one'. Points of
musical grammar which were discussed as a result were
chords, widespread chords (aural space), gaps between notes
(intervals), clashes (dissonance), notes which go together
(consonance), going off the note slightly up or down (singing
flat or sharp). After hearing the bells two boys were absorbed in
making the most vibrating noise on a cymbal, one of them
most carefully controlling his hitting while the other put his
ear closely underneath to hear the vibrations. Children are
intensely curious about vibration and deeply absorbed in its
effects; their early activity in music genuinely constitutes a
scientific exploring and experimenting with sound. 'Vibration'
is almost the first term to be used in connection with musical
activity: 'I can feel the vibrations.'; 'The floor is vibrating.';
'My drum is vibrating.'

A boy (7.4) produced this pattern on two drums while his
partner played a continuous drum roll; both players knelt on
the floor with their instruments in front of them. As soon as the
players began other children gathered round fascinated by the
sight of the playing. Others joined the group not because they
had seen the movement of the players but because the sound at
once evoked a recognitive response and an expectation. Their

musical experience was such that they knew the technique was going to be interesting to watch. The experience of the boy who was playing was such that he *knew* his idea would work well; he had a belief in his own ability and in the potential effect of the technique and instruments he had selected (see Chapter 9). Three times he stopped because he had gone wrong, his partner stopping and starting with him. After the third attempt he wiped his forehead saying, 'It's *so* difficult.' The fourth attempt was successful. The music was given unity and coherence by the repetition four times of the rhythm scheme. His partner at no time played too loudly, keeping firmly to his role of accompanist (see Chapter 8). Other children's work was based on this for several weeks afterwards; it had been inspiring.

Clearly this musical activity reflected the conservation of basic musical ideas which had taken place: pulse, groupings of four beats, rests, rhythm pattern, roll, main part and accompaniment. The thinking was reversible. This boy had reached the stage of operational thinking within the musical discipline.

These last examples trace the development of banging, illustrating its metamorphosis through phases of random hitting and deliberate aim to the point where it becomes instrumental technique and the cause of good instrumental tone. This early mode of causing sound is often applied to new material of which hitting is not the culturally developed technique. It is perhaps surprising that young children should approach a cello, or more particularly a guitar, with a beater, having inevitably viewed much playing of it on television. One teacher frequently observed this mode of behaviour in groups of children of six and seven as they experimented in making sounds on different types of string instruments: violin, cello, guitar, banjo, autoharp, chordal zither, chordal dulcimer. Their awareness of string technique and tone grew because the very unsatisfactoriness of the mode of causing sound posed the problem of finding a better way. They were helped by listening to some older children playing instruments, but not until their *own* activity was perceived by them to be limited and ineffectual on the particular material chosen did they experiment with other ways of causing sound, plucking with fingers, for example, and, when fingers were sore, using pluckers (plectrums), or music which exists in our culture. It is very unlikely that children will develop in this way if their early experience of music is of playing in a group chosen by the teacher, of being told what to do, when to play, how to hold the instrument and of following a score before they have any real understanding of what the notational symbols represent. This too often becomes a purely rote activity in which the appearance of children playing instruments and seemingly actively involved deceives us into thinking that they are genuinely involved in music making. What is involved in group music making? The wish to do so and the ability to do so are both essential. The ability to do so develops as the basic conceptual structure of musical ideas is established when ideas are held in common and are therefore communicable. In the previous examples it was the older children who chose to work together, discussing their parts as they planned their music. They were co-operating, they understood each other's ideas and were able to adapt their own ideas to a common aim, the creation of a piece of music. It is this sort of communication and co-operation which is later essential in ensemble work and orchestral playing.

> Two girls (6) were playing at the same time; both were causing sound simultaneously but they were not aware of each other's music and in no way worked together. One player did not realize that her sound was being drowned by the other, and when one stopped it was some time before the other noticed that she was playing alone.

This inability to view their activity from the outside is characteristic of many children of six and seven. Each child's focus is on his activity: his view is egocentric.

> Three boys in the same group were eventually forced to end their music which had gone on and on and on, by shouts of 'Stop!' from all over the room.
>
> Four six-year-old girls in the same group *were* co-operating in a very concentrated manner, watching each other all the time. They each played crotchets ♩♩♩♩ on a number of instruments and managed to keep perfectly in time with each other, accommodating to a tempo not necessarily their own

bowing the open strings of a violin, not necessarily held under the chin but perhaps flat on the floor, at first with hard scraping and very squeaky results. Finally, discussions about the 'proper' ways of playing the different instruments became frequent. The glissando is another early mode of causing sound which is at first used indiscriminately on pitch instruments, even on recorders and melodicas. The perception of the long shape of the xylophone causes the direct action of banging (as on a drum) to be modified. The movement is extended and ceases to be direct, an element of flexibility developing in the ending flourish (see Chapter 5). It is a simple enough matter for the teacher to find out from books or from visiting instrumentalists what are the accepted techniques, and a matter of intelligent observation to assess the stage of the child's development in relation to these techniques. Being with young children is inevitably a learning situation for teachers too, and if they are willing to experiment with instrumental noises themselves, their own activity will illuminate their observations of the children.

Instrumental provision is obviously most important if children are to develop ideas of technique and tone. In making this provision two factors must be taken into account. First, the way the sound is made—notes *and* chords hit, scraped, plucked, blown or fingered, and second, the pitch range of the instrument. Many children have experience of tinkly glockenspiels and of small not very resonant tambourines, but not of low string or wind tone or the sound of a bass drum. Experience of notes in bass and treble sounding both successively and simultaneously is essential for the subsequent development of concepts of harmony. In consideration of these two factors, a third is inevitably taken into account: that of timbre (particular tone quality). That children's aural perception will develop from making music with objects like tins and bottles is certain, but as the musical potential of such things is limited so inevitably will be the children's development. Collecting a wide range of instruments is not always an expensive enterprise; there are all sorts of instruments to be found in junk shops whose tone is quite acceptable and whose repair if necessary is not difficult.

Two aspects of the provision of a musical environment have

been discussed: songs and instruments. There also exists a wealth of music easily available on record for children to hear. It is important that musical criteria and not personal preferences be taken into account in the selection of recorded music so that the children be given the opportunity for as wide a range of hearing experience as possible. Elementary classifications are of value here in ensuring this wide range: classification according to composer, period of musical history, the form of the music and the forces employed in it (whether it is written for full orchestra or smaller group of instruments, for voices and orchestra, etc.).

School assemblies are enhanced by the opportunity for children to listen to music, particularly if the time for listening is not arbitrarily decided in advance but depends from day to day on the concentration span of the children. It is appropriate to children's needs that music should be faded out when they have had enough listening: it is also appropriate from the point of view of the music as no purpose is served in enforced listening. We know that enforced listening causes ears and minds to be shut and becomes not listening at all, doing little to recommend listening to music. On the other hand, we tend to underestimate children's capacity both in their concentration span where the interest is strong and in their response to styles of music to which many adults have difficulty in listening.

A stimulating environment of songs, records and instruments is of little value without the provision of opportunity for children to work with them. The teacher is presented with the problem of creating a situation in which children are free to explore and discover and experiment for themselves with musical things, and one in which they are free to make up their own music in the mode of working appropriate to their stage of development. This may be random hitting or intentional organization of pitch or a highly organized trio, or quartet (in which beginning and ending are clearly planned, in which a main theme is played by each part in turn or together, or in which each part has its own theme). It must, too, be a situation in which they are free *not* to make up music if their present interest lies elsewhere. None of the difficulties of school organization or noise level must be allowed to outweigh children's need to learn about the musical aspect of the world in which they live in the way

that they learn about everything else. One solution would be to split the classes, one half having their music time two or three times in the week at least, while the other half were busy elsewhere. It is unlikely that many schools will have enough equipment for classes of forty children all to use instruments at the same time: it is also unlikely that the school society would have enough aural resilience for this!

It may be that music is the responsibility of one teacher in the school, who teaches it more happily than anyone else, and then all the musical apparatus is likely to be centred in one room. In this room would be housed in cupboards or trolleys a collection of instruments adequate for the purpose of twenty children all making music at the same time. These instruments would be spread out on tables in preparation for a music work session to avoid any unnecessary scramble as twenty children made their choice of instrument(s) with which to work. On the other hand, individual class teachers may be expected to take their own music with perhaps rather meagre instrumental provision in each room. The room will probably have a music table or corner, the number of children working there at any one time being limited by the selection of instruments available, and the times of day for music work limited to a certain extent to ensure that there are periods in the room when children can work quietly without the noise of music to disturb them. In these schools music may not be time-tabled at all but treated as a part of the general class activity. An adequate supply of instruments (criteria of selection being taken into account would be housed in a music corner probably containing cupboard or trolley and tables.

However the music time is organized, it must revolve ro the work of the children. There must be time and opportu for them to choose an instrument, to choose a partner or g or not, to make up some music, to record it in a book need is felt, and subsequently to perform it to the class wish. The only way in which young children first I aware of the problems in their environment is in task they have set themselves. Furthermore it is the basic s of ideas developed in this way which later enable ch approach externally set problems successfully, and to construe the intention of the composer in interp

in the first place. One of the group looked hard at the others when she judged it appropriate to end. Her judgment was a correct one as the audience was still absorbed in material which held their interest.

A look or a nudge is often the first mode of bringing group playing to an end, and is much enjoyed for its own sake! When ideas are developing in young children their behaviour often reflects a state of flux until an equilibrium is achieved.

A group of six-year-old boys co-operated successfully in playing drums; patches of regular beats developed *during* the activity. The leader looked meaningly at the others and mouthed 'stop'. He played a definite ending bang. So did each of his two friends and this went on for quite some time, to the great amusement of the class. One of them said, 'We *all* wanted to have the last bang.' This argument of beats delighted the players and similar behaviour continued until the idea of ending a piece of music satisfactorily became so clear and important that it prevailed over their enjoyment of the game.

These children were building up their ideas about discipline in the creation of a coherent musical statement. As social co-operation develops the planning of the music becomes more and more important, and more verbal. Last minute consultations before the performance occur very frequently and it becomes a challenge to keep to the plan. The music played in performance at first often bears no resemblance to the music played in the working time. Until a conceptual framework begins to develop, children cannot possibly *know* what they are doing but as their ideas grow and they begin to work with somebody else planning becomes important. It is this planning which leads ultimately to an understanding and knowledge of form in music and an ability to operate within it. If teachers are not certain of their own musical knowledge it is a simple enough matter for them to find out about form in music and to analyse children's activity in relation to it. There are books which set out in the language of common sense the ideas concerning the organization of musical material which have evolved over the centuries, and there are broadcasts intended to help adults understand the musical discipline more fully.

Just as the child's planning of his music leads ultimately to
his understanding of musical form, so his selection of instruments
leads toward his understanding of orchestration. If young
children are free to choose the instruments they work with they
learn how to choose, and how to exercise judgment in the
selection of material suitable to their purpose.

> A boy (4) crossed the room and played the glockenspiel. He
> did not cross the room because he had decided to play it, he
> played it because his wandering across the room happened
> to end in front of a shelf holding a glockenspiel. If different
> instruments had been left on the shelf the musical result would
> have been different.
>
> The boys in a group of six-year-olds considered one drum
> (quite rightly) to be the best in the room; there was great
> competition to get it first. But no-one was very disturbed not to
> get it, and another instrument was happily taken instead. At
> their stage of development the action of playing took precedence
> over anything else. A girl (6) searched in all the instrument
> boxes for a harmonica. 'I'm playing with Mary [also with a
> harmonica] and we want to go together.'
>
> A boy (7) chose a drum until he could play it to his satisfaction.
> A group of girls (7) collected as many instruments as they could
> setting them out on tables in front of them. Faced with playing
> such an array they could not make musical sense. Someone
> remarked, 'It was rather chaotic because they had too many
> instruments.'

Many children at this stage collect an array of instruments;
they have a growing awareness of the particular sound quality
of individual instruments (instrumental colour), of the effect
of various combinations of instruments and of the need for
variety. Comments such as 'I don't like those instruments
together', or 'Those instruments don't go well together' or
'I would have chosen another instrument to go with the guitar',
occur frequently in discussion. A concern that every instrument
should be heard grows: 'The drum drowned the glockenspiel'
or 'I couldn't hear the guitar.' Gradually ideas develop about
the use of contrasting and similar tone, about the total effect
of the individual parts and about the unique expressiveness of
each instrument and its appropriate material.

Until the basic musical ideas are established there can be no possible understanding of any notational symbols representing these ideas. To present these symbols to children prematurely can damage their later potential understanding of them, as it forces them to operate in a meaningless way, recapturing the notes instead of re-living the understanding. It is significant that in several groups of nine and ten-year-olds, the children with most difficulty and reluctance in writing and reading music were those who had been taught the piano before they had reached the stage of a genuine understanding of simple musical ideas. To write music (to score it) involves an analytical understanding of your own intention: to read music it is necessary to construe the composer's intention. For these activities to be understood an analysis of the rhythm, the pitch, the tempo, the dynamics, the mood, the style, the necessary technique is essential. Such an analysis can only result from an understanding of the ideas involved. Indeed, it is when these ideas become well established that children begin to feel a need to make a written record of their music. The idea for the music is so clear that they feel a wish to remember it exactly, and as memory is not always reliable, a score must be made. This also enables other people to play the music. At first symbols are used from existing ideas of graphic representation, of space, density, number, letters. It is a matter of delicate judgment for the teacher to present to the child the correct symbol within musical notation either at her own suggestion or at the request 'What is the proper way to write a glissando?' or 'How do I put a crescendo?' (see Figures 1–7).

Children's paintings, models and constructions are put on view so that the rest of the class may see and enjoy them, discuss and learn from them. It is important that children's music should be heard by their group or class and that they should have experience of playing music to people who are listening. Getting ready for performance time after a working session involves careful arranging of instruments and beaters so that they are easily to hand and unlikely to drop and disturb someone else's playing. As their experience of involvement in music grows a sense of commitment to it also grows and they become absorbed in other people's music as well as their own. This becomes apparent in the behaviour of seven-year-olds. An emotional sensibility to the language of music grows both through giving performances and receiving them (see Chapter 3). At times a piece of music may evoke a deeply felt silence or appreciative comments: 'How lovely!' or 'It was beautiful!' or 'It made me feel...!' It may evoke delighted recognition and bursting enthusiasm: '*How* could he do it?' or 'It was *so* good' or 'I *loved* that' or 'That really was music'. At other times an analytical discussion may follow: 'It had a good beat', 'They kept in time', 'I don't think they had planned it at all', 'I wouldn't have put a bang at the end', 'She made a very good sound on the xylophone', 'It was all made up of glissandos', 'It was too repeating', 'They shouldn't have gone on so long, it got boring', 'I think they could repeat it', 'He made an accelerando', 'She played scales up and down', 'They all kept to their own rhythm'. All these comments were made by seven and eight-year-olds after listening to other children's work. Here the teacher's contribution is crucial. By joining the discussion with comments and questions, finely judged, she can bring to children's notice both the ideas they themselves have used in their music and the ideas that other children have used. 'Why?', 'What do you mean?', 'What would you have done?', 'Did you notice so-and so?', 'The proper musical term for what you did is . . .', 'Lots of music does that—the parts entering one after the other' and so on. These questions and comments bring children's activity to a conscious level and such discussions foster the development of musical thinking.

Music has its life in the mutual response of the maker and the hearer. We value this response and greatly esteem those who evoke it by their composition or performance. Our life is enriched by a few extraordinarily gifted people who become a creative force in our musical culture. Only a very small percentage of the population is so gifted. At the other pole, a universal musical response is evident in the activity of very young children. Faced with a disturbing level of musical illiteracy in our society we are forced to acknowledge that, either by its action or inaction, society causes this response to shrivel and die. Indeed in society we are in the conflicting situation of being the cause of deprivation of a response which we value highly. Musicians and educators are aware of this and have been concerned with the teaching of musical skills to the young: instrumental expertise, fluent reading, aural training. More recently a concern that music should be a creative activity has arisen, but the term has been loosely and confusingly used and genuine creativity has not necessarily followed. Somehow the devotion has failed the cause, and musical education for the most part is an inhibitory process which fails to tap the capacity for musical response and development and the potential creativeness which are inherent in the human organism. By looking at the musical response so evident in the activity of young children we are shown how musical development begins. We have to take it from there and, by joining the mainstream of their development, nurture the growth of musical ideas. Children's improvisation and composition will gradually help them to understand the significance of musical constructions, of thematic development, of the relationship between the judicious use of device and expressive power, of the use of motif or cluster (set of notes). It is through the gradual development of their individual and personal world of music that they will find the key to the wider world of music as established in our culture pattern.

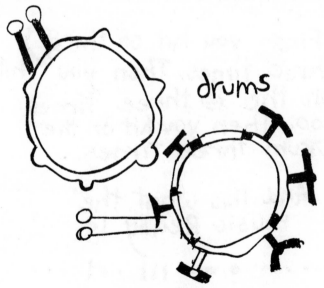

Figure 1   Boy, 6.6
At first, drawings of the instruments used represent the music played.

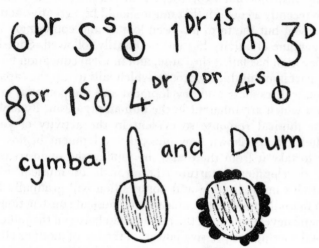

Figures 2, 3   Seven-year-old girls

These children are using their own notation, with a clear explanation to make sure that it is not misunderstood.

First you hit on the ⊛ three times. Then you ⊛ hit on the ⊚ three times too. Then you hit on the Drum three times.

And this what the music Really is.

··· ••• ||| •·| ···
••• ||| •·•·•|·|•|

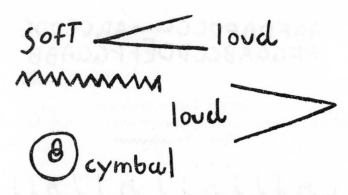

Figure 4   Seven-year-old girl   〜〜〜 = a roll

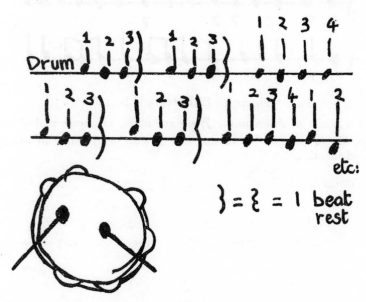

Figure 5   Eight-year-old girl

Both these children are beginning to use correct notational symbols; their intention is clear.

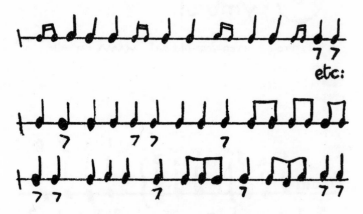

Figure 6   Eight-year-old girl

Music for xylophone using alphabetical note names with the correct sign for a glissando in the first line ⌇⌇⌇⌇.

Figure 7   Eight-year-old boys

Two pieces of drum music; ♫ = grace notes, i.e. notes played as quickly as possible before the beat; ꜛ = an accent, i.e. an extra loud sound.

CHAPTER 8

Morality: Values and Reasons

A YOUNG woman who inherited some money asked her bank manager how she should invest it. As he advised her she realized that she was beginning to understand for the first time the principle of compound interest, although at school she had done many compound interest sums correctly. This example illustrates the distinction that Whitehead has made between knowledge which remains inert and unapplied, and knowledge which is dynamic and is applied to relevant problems. The distinction is educationally important in any subject, but most people could 'get by' without having learned the principle of compound interest. In the area of morality on the other hand, even if 'getting by' were possible, it would be most undesirable, for our moral behaviour constantly affects both our own lives and those of others.

Moral development is concerned with both moral behaviour and moral judgment, and a mature, rational morality is one in which moral judgments result in moral behaviour, and, vice versa, in which behaviour in the moral area is based on rational moral judgment. A kind of inert knowledge exists in the moral area when a judgment is made about a situation, but the appropriate behaviour does not necessarily follow from the judgment. In other words, there are moral lapses, which we all experience at some time or another, and which occur whenever we fail to subordinate our selfish desires to what we know is morally right. Thus moral development consists in part in the growing ability to put the common good before the selfish one, to live by moral principles of justice, loyalty, integrity, responsibility and respect for persons, which transcend personal gain.

The gradual differentiation between 'self' and 'others' is therefore an important ingredient in moral development. This differentiation begins in infancy as a baby gradually learns that objects and people have a permanent existence which is independent of his own activity. This construction of the idea of the permanence of objects, which had been described in previous chapters, marks the first major step in this differentiation between self and others.

In the pre-school years the continuing development of self-awareness involves a move from anonymity to person which is demonstrated in the use of language: from 'go', 'Peter go', 'me go', to 'I go'.

At the same time a characteristic which Piaget calls egocentricity, and which has been described in previous chapters, marks the pre-school years and continues into the first school years. Egocentricity is not synonymous with selfishness. The latter implies that one's own desires and purposes are placed above those of other people: it involves ignoring the wishes of others even while understanding what these might be. Egocentricity in this sense implies that a child is intellectually unable to put himself at another person's point of view; it is not so much that he ignores the interests of others as that he does not understand what these are. Egocentricity results in social behaviour which may look selfish to adult eyes, but which arises from this inability to put himself in another's place. A boy aged four years seven months remarked, when it started to rain immediately on their arrival at a camping site, 'God sent the rain so no-one else would come to our camp.' This child's idea of God as an indulgent power committed to the gratification of his personal desires illustrates the egocentricity of this stage of development: he was not yet able to put himself in other people's positions in order to think of their needs and wishes in terms of both weather and access to the camping site.

At this stage of egocentricity there may be a superficial appearance of 'give and take', of co-operation, but only where children's purposes are in harmony. Where there is a conflict of purposes apparent co-operation breaks down because the necessary accommodation by one child to another child's point of view is not possible. Thus in the nursery school there can be a measure of co-operation between a group of children pushing a large truck if they all want to push it, but conflict arises when more than one of them want to ride in a truck which holds only one child. Or there is co-operation in their 'home play' when one child wants to be 'mother' and the other 'the child', but when they both want to be 'mother' either there is conflict or the situation resolved by their both being 'mothers' and there is then parallel rather than co-operative play.

Although in these years children are limited in their ability to 'think' themselves into another person's position or point of view, they do learn to recognize other people's experiences as similar to their own, and this leads to real sympathy and a quasi co-operation. It is quite common for a child in the nursery school, who has been watching a new entrant crying, to say sympathetically, 'He is crying because he wants his mother'. A five-year-old, who sees the collapse of the carefully constructed brick model of another five-year-old and offers to help him to rebuild it, may be quite unable to put himself at the other child's point of view when it is different from his own, but in this situation he knows the other child's feelings about the collapse of his model because he himself has experienced similar feelings in similar situations. There is a growing sensitivity to other people's feelings because children's increasing self-awareness enables them to identify similar expressions of feelings in others.

The behaviour of the important adults in children's lives is a crucial factor in this aspect of development. If a child was comforted by the teacher when, as a new entrant to school he was distressed at leaving his mother, if he was helped when some valued construction collapsed, then comfort and help are part of his total experiences. In assimilating another child's feelings to his own he is more likely to offer comfort and help if these were part of his own experience. The growth of self-awareness is helped too by consistent treatment from adults and hindered by inconsistency. A child who is rebuked for behaviour for which he was previously praised by the same adult has fewer stable points of reference from which he can evaluate experiences than a child who receives more consistent treatment.

As is suggested in Chapter 4 one of the functions of stories for young children is a recognitive one. Where experiences familiar to a child are presented in a story in recognizable form they increase self-awareness.

The decrease in egocentricity through the first school years means that children become progressively able to understand situations from points of view different from their own. An eight-year-old girl, who heard her mother complain about the frequent uninvited visits of a neighbour, remarked, 'You ought not to say that. She doesn't go out to work like you, so she doesn't have interests like you do.' This represents a considerable growth in complexity of understanding about other people's feelings and experiences compared with the egocentric position of the four-year-old boy quoted above. This growth through the first school years means that children become increasingly able to accommodate to other children's wishes and ideas as well as to assimilate them to their own: they not only recognize the feelings and ideas of others when they are similar to their own experiences, but they also gradually learn to put themselves at the point of view of others even when that point of view is different from their own. True co-operation and sharing become possible.

There is no sudden change from egocentricity to co-operation. Egocentricity diminishes gradually through the first school years, and there are, of course, individual developmental differences between children. A child's ability to 'think' himself into the position of another person appears gradually in different situations and in relation to different problems. It is an ability that is partly dependent on the experiences a child has had. These experiences involve opportunities for co-operation, for the ability to co-operate depends in part on the opportunities a child has had of co-operating. Children begin to appreciate that other people may have ideas and wishes which are different from and may even conflict with their own, and they begin to understand what these wishes and ideas are through social experiences where ideas are exchanged and where true co-operation can only be achieved by resolving the problems created by opposing ideas and wishes.

A first school which provides many opportunities for co-operative activities will maximize experiences that are vital to this aspect of moral growth. As previous chapters have shown, certain activities like dramatic play, musical experimentation and movement, in particular, lead naturally from individual to group activity. Co-operation grows from common pursuits and is gradually therefore seen by children to be a valuable basis for the extension of ideas.

One of the advantages of 'vertical grouping' in the first school may be that it creates many opportunities for co-operation between children. A mixed age group makes it possible for children to benefit and learn from the more mature, while the older children themselves find opportunities to develop qualities of sensitivity and responsibility toward the younger children. It would seem particularly helpful for the younger children, for the immaturity of a class of five-year-olds makes it more difficult for them to learn from and with each other.

By contrast, competitive situations can militate against the development of co-operation. Competition can undermine co-operation and hinder moral growth when it leads to the categorization of some individuals as 'inferior' and some as 'superior'. It thus consistently weakens the self-confidence of some children and incorporates ideas of inadequacy into their growing concepts of self. Their capacity to interact positively and constructively with other children, particularly with children categorized as 'superior', is diminished. The prognosis is equally bleak for those children who are categorized as 'superior' within a competitive system. Moral growth is concerned not only with understanding another person's point of view, but also with caring about that point of view. Subordinating the gratification of one's own desires and interests to those of another person when it is morally proper to do so is more difficult if one does not care about the desires and interests of the other person. Caring is cultivated when each child is treated with respect and valued for whatever contributions he is capable of making to the life of the classroom community; it is undermined by the devaluing of children which results from categorizing them as inferior. Children do, of course, become increasingly aware of differences between themselves, and it is right that they should do so, for this is an integral part of their growing powers of intellectual discrimination. What is insidious in moral growth is a gross valuation in terms of 'inferior' and 'superior' on the basis of these differences. Competitive classroom organizations often go hand in hand with arbitrarily imposed 'rewards' such as stars or house points. These deflect a child's attention from

intrinsic to extrinsic criteria, and militate against his valuing
his own real achievements or those of other children.

The introduction of pets into the classroom may be important
for young children, in that the cultivation of the ability to care
for other persons may well be helped by experience in caring
for animals. For young children at the egocentric stage of
development, caring for other persons may well be difficult
when the complexity and variety of human behaviour makes it
unpredictable, whereas by contrast the response of animals is
simpler, apparently more stable, and therefore more pre-
dictable.

The gradual release from egocentricity includes the increasing ability of a child to consider another child's ideas, and
as a result to reconsider and modify his own where appropriate.
The development of language both in vocabulary and syntax
plays an important part in both the understanding and communication of ideas. Indeed, some behaviour difficulties are
due to inadequate or inaccurate understanding of the language
used, particularly if the children are immigrants or have poor
language development.

> One teacher, when wanting her class of forty children to listen
> to her, was accustomed to say, 'Please listen everybody.' Most
> of the children would stop what they were doing, but two or
> three consistently ignored this request and would continue
> their activity and talking. This behaviour puzzled the teacher,
> for they were not disobedient at other times, and she asked them
> what 'everybody' meant. Their reply was, 'All of them',
> pointing to the other children. When she explained that it
> meant 'all of them—and you' the difficulty was solved.

Teachers have a vital role to play in helping children to
acquire language which will help them in communicating and
crystallizing their experiences, and in categorizing various
aspects of moral behaviour. The following examples from a
teacher's record book were collected over several days and show
how one seven-year-old girl was trying to come to an understanding of the meaning of kindness:

> 1. 'It was kind of Jane to say to Denise's mummy that she
> would bring Denise down the drive to school'.
> Teacher: 'Why was it kind?'

'Well, Denise's mummy might be going to be busy, so it would save her time if Jane brought Denise down the drive.'
2. 'It was kind of Nicole to undo the knot in my shoelace.'
3. 'It was kind of Andrea to write that word for me when you weren't there.'
4. Conversation at lunch time: 'It was kind of Miss H. to bring you your pudding.'

This series of examples represents only those comments noted by the teacher. There may well have been other occasions unknown to her when this child made similar attempts to test out, clarify and question what actions came within the categories of kindness and unkindness. They show how the child was concentrating on this specific moral quality and using a wide range of situations and social contacts in coming to an understanding.

It was stated above that moral lapses occur when moral judgment does not result in moral behaviour; when a person can judge what is right and proper, but out of self-interest acts in a way contrary to his judgment. There is another sort of inert knowledge in the area of morals, which also leads to moral immaturity of a different kind. This is the moral immaturity that stems from the reverse position when there is behaviour which at a casual glance appears moral, but which is not the outcome of mature moral judgment. In order to understand this, a differentiation must be made between standards of behaviour and moral values. Standards are overt: they constitute the observable consistent behaviour displayed by a person in relation to similar situations. A person, for example, who is always hospitable to his friends and acquaintances, whenever they call, can be said to exhibit high standards of hospitality. Values, on the other hand, are internal: they constitute a relatively stable system representing the worth given by an individual to certain principles. Standards should be the external expression of this internal system which we call values. Thus the standards of hospitality referred to above should be an expression of the value attached by the host to his friends and to friendship. But this connection is by no means a necessary one, and it is possible for certain standards to be a matter of custom rather than the expression of the relevant values.

A mature, rational morality means that standards are the expression of a person's moral value system. Such a one acts loyally because he values loyalty, he behaves with responsibility because he values duty, and he treats all persons with respect because respect for persons is part of his value system. A morally immature person may be one in whom this connection between standards and values does not exist: although he appears to behave 'correctly', his behaviour is more a matter of custom than an expression of moral values. A person who demonstrates high standards of politeness in face-to-face situations, but who then spreads malicious gossip concerning the very people to whom he has been polite, indicates that his polite behaviour is not rooted in the appropriate values.

Standards which are not based on values are not truly moral. They are frequently exhibited in certain specific situations only and not generalized beyond them. This specificity which characterizes standards not based on values is particularly undesirable in an open society such as ours. An open society, as distinct from a closed one, demands flexible and generalized standards if these are to be applied in the complex situations and the great variety of groups that are found in an open society.

Truly moral behaviour, as distinct from such conditioned imitation of custom, involves intention and deliberation. It is relatively easy for young children to learn such words as 'sorry' or 'thank you' without understanding. This was demonstrated in a situation which developed among a group of four- and five-year-olds playing on a slide. One girl was much more skilful than the others, and was able to speed up her running and sliding so that she overtook other children. She became rough as she pushed past with increasing speed, and finally a child fell crying to the ground. She was picked up by one of the group who took her to the teacher and explained what had happened. The teacher came out to the playground, and without questioning the offender chastised her and said, 'Say you're sorry to J.' The child was reluctant but eventually placed her hands mechanically on the other child's shoulders and mumbled 'Sorry.' This child may have learned that under pressure it is necessary to repeat words spoken by an adult, or she may have learned to use the word as an act of appeasement. She certainly did not learn to connect the word with the feeling of sorrow, for this was clearly not the feeling she was experiencing at that moment. It would have been morally more educative if the teacher had helped this child to understand the feelings of the other child, and then, perhaps, to have given her the appropriate word and gesture.

Standards have been defined above in terms of consistent behaviour. No person can be said to be morally mature if his standards are inconsistent and unpredictable. But consistency is not synonymous with inflexibility, and, while consistency is desirable, there is a certain sort of inflexibility which is not. Flexibility is necessary to resolve the moral problems which occur whenever we are faced with a situation which involves making a choice between conflicting moral issues. For example, a conflict arises between equality and fairness, when to treat people equally might result in an unfairness being done to a person or persons. Professional people are sometimes faced with a conflict between a personal and a professional loyalty. A principle concerned with the sanctity of other people's property might need to be abandoned in a situation of emergency involving the risk of life or limb of another human being. Children at the upper end of the first school, who are beginning to develop a sense of loyalty toward their peers, are often faced with conflict between this loyalty and loyalty to an adult. Moral maturity means the ability to resolve such conflicts, and demands that the resolution is rational and not arbitrary. A rational resolution demands a set of moral principles which are hierarchically structured and which it is here claimed puts respect for persons first.

It is also possible to exhibit standards which are not simply conditioned custom, but which are still not based on such a system of moral values. They are rather the outcome of a rigid set of rules which have been accepted from some authority without having been thought through sufficiently to have become structured into a hierarchical system of moral values. A code of this sort may be generalized and not have the specificity of standards which are the result of conditioned custom, but it will not have the flexibility necessary to the resolution of moral conflict. For example, a rule about the sanctity of private property may be generalized to include all persons' property, but it is rigid if it cannot be abandoned in the face of human distress because it cannot be subordinated to a principle concerned with respect for persons. A rigid code of this sort does not include the flexibility necessary to the rational resolution of moral conflict and therefore cannot be a sufficient basis for a rational morality. As John Wilson [52] says:

> The degree to which an action or a belief is rational is connected with how far they are really *our own:* that is, how far they are the result of our facing facts and responding freely, rather than compulsively, to them. In so far as our actions approximate to mere reactive or reflex movement, and our belief to sets of words which are merely parroted or accepted solely on authority, to that extent we fall away from acting and thinking as moral agents.

A rational morality in our view is therefore one involving moral judgments based on reasons, which are an integral part of a moral value system hierarchically structured in a rational way where the principle of respect for persons is placed at the top of the hierarchy. It defines a mature morality which should be seen as the ultimate objective of moral education.

The development of moral judgment in children has been investigated and described by Piaget [39]. He explored children's judgments about situations involving, for example, lying, stealing, disobeying parental commands and causing damage, and by questioning them on suitable punishments in these situations he exposed their ideas of justice and fairness. The situations about which he questioned the children were recounted in pairs of stories which involved the same misdemeanour but differed in terms of intention or motive, and in terms of the extent of the misdemeanour from a purely objective point of view. The following is a pair of stories concerned with lying:

> A. A little boy goes for a walk in the street and meets a dog who frightens him very much. So then he goes home and tells his mother he has seen a dog that was as big as a cow.
> B. A child comes home from school and tells his mother that the teacher had given him good marks, but it was not true; the teacher had given him no marks at all, either good or bad.

Another pair of stories was concerned with stealing:

- A. Alfred meets a little friend of his who is very poor. This friend tells him that he has had no dinner that day because there was nothing to eat in his home. Then Alfred goes into a baker's shop, and as he has no money he waits till the baker's back is turned and steals a roll. Then he runs out and gives the roll to his friend.
- B. Henriette goes into a shop. She sees a pretty piece of ribbon on a table and thinks to herself that it would look nice on her dress. So while the shop lady's back is turned she steals the ribbon and runs away at once.

Piaget found that children's ideas about these and other similar situations could be described as going through certain stages. The first major stage is the 'morality of constraint', so-called because at this stage children's judgments seem to be constrained by rules, which they conceive to be those of adult authority, and which they interpret in an absolutist way. The second major stage is the 'morality of co-operation', so-called because children's judgments are now more democratic and flexible, and develop through interaction with their peers. The ages at which children's ideas go through these stages show a wide variation and there is variation too in any one child's judgments in relation to different situations, but the stage of morality of contraint lasts roughly until seven or eight years. Thus most of the children in the first school will be at this stage in at least some areas to do with moral judgment. At the stage of morality of constraint children judge the exaggerated story about the encounter with the 'dog as big as a cow' to be a more serious offence than the lie about good marks in school. Their judgments are based on the fact that the former is a 'taller story.' Motives are ignored and the fact that the second mother was likely to be deceived by the more plausible lie is not taken into account, and neither is the fear of the first child, which might have led him to overestimate the size of the dog. Similarly in the second pair of stories the fact that the motives of the one child were well intentioned and those of the other were selfish is ignored by children at the stage of morality of constraint. By questioning children on punishments in various situations Piaget also found that at the stage of morality of constraint children tend to think of punishment as an expiation.

The more severe the punishment the fairer they think it is. Children who have reached the second more mature stage of morality of co-operation tend to believe that punishment should follow the principle of reciprocity. Severity is not necessary: punishment should simply restore the status quo. At the earlier stage of development children tend to regard rules as emanating from authority and as sacrosanct and unchangeable. At the next stage, on the other hand, they believe that it is possible to change rules and make others, providing that this is done in a fair and democratic way.

Piaget's findings would indicate that much of adult moralizing in terms of motives and consequences to children at the stage of morality of constraint is of little meaning to them. But there are arguments to show that giving them a set of recommendations or precepts without reasons, on the grounds that at this stage they have difficulty in understanding the justification of moral principles and regard rules as sacrosanct, is equally undesirable.

Firstly, as Williams [52] points out, Piaget has frequently insisted that he does not regard stages as discontinuities. He sees development as a continuous process in which each stage is dependent on the preceding stage and integrated into the succeeding one. This would imply that, although experiences of interacting with their peers are vital to the development of children's understanding of rules and their ideas of fairness and justice, the quality of their experience of adult authority and adult morality is of equal consequence. Adults provide models of possible behaviour in their treatment of children. A parent or teacher, who apologizes when she accidentally knocks over a child's possession, or who takes into account a child's own motives as she judges his behaviour, puts the child in a position to assimilate positive attitudes to accident which can form the raw material of his own future behaviour. Similarly, rudeness to children or lack of concern will influence their future actions. (The extent to which a child can make judgments which take motives into account will be influenced by his own experiences.) A young child is dependent on adults in building up a store of possible actions, and the cumulative effect of positive or negative responses will inevitably influence the quality of his actions.

Secondly, Piaget's explanation of intellectual development includes the concept of the human organism actively exploring the environment and organizing his experience. There would seem to be no logical reason why moral ideas should be in a different category in the earlier years of life, arising only through the passive acceptance of adult recommendations, and not including any active attempt at understanding the reasons for them. Observation does in fact indicate that young children do try to understand the rules and edicts of adults. In the development of language the nature of the questions children ask gives an indication of the nature of their intellectual explorations at any one period. Some of children's earliest questions, often beginning with 'what', are attempts to identify and to categorize objects and situations in a simple way. Some questions of this type are related to parent's rules and prohibitions.

> A two-year-old girl whose parents had a fine collection of objets d'art had been told not to touch something 'because it is an antique'. Whenever anything new was bought she asked, 'Is it an antique?' Another two-year-old was told not to touch the cooker because 'It is dangerous and will hurt you'. During the next few days she systematically asked of a variety of objects, especially those which emitted heat like the iron and the toaster, 'Is it dangerous?'

Later, between three and four years of age, children begin to ask questions beginning with 'Why', which seek not just to identify but also to explain events. As Nathan Isaacs [22] points out in his analysis of children's 'why' questions, many of these are concerned with adult motives and purposes and indicate that they are seeking the reasons for rules and often for some simple moral principle: 'The "why" question thus comes to aim not merely at any sort of familiar motive or purpose for the rule, but at a ground or justification which will make it clear what there is to make this rule necessary or desirable.'

Thirdly, it should be remembered that Piaget explored children's moral judgments by questioning them about situations which were not concerned directly with their own experiences although they may have had similar ones. It is

probable that in this, as in other aspects of intellectual development, children judge at a higher level in relation to experiences
to which they have given consideration because they are their
own.

> A seven-year-old acquaintance returned from his friend's tea
> party pre-occupied with the fact that another boy had eaten
> so many cakes that none was left for the host's older sister.
> After stating that the boy had been very greedy he reconsidered
> the problem and said, 'But perhaps he could not help it, be-
> cause his mother has left him and perhaps his father has not
> taught him not to be greedy. So it's really his father's fault.'
> There then followed some reconsideration and he modified
> this notion. 'Perhaps it was not his father's fault, because his
> father had not taught him either. Perhaps it was his father's
> father who was the first one to say, 'I'm deliberately going to
> be greedy.'

Embedded in this simple, child-like statement is a notion, which
is most sophisticated for a seven-year-old child, involving the
relationship of responsibility to knowledge and intention.

In the first school teachers can help in laying the foundations
for a rational morality by attempting to get children to understand the justifications for rules. Justifications are reasons
which are rational rather than arbitrary. 'Because I said so'
is a reason for not shouting in the corridor but not a rational
justification for the rule, whereas 'because it interferes with the
freedom of other children and teachers to listen to other things'
is a rational justification. There are rules which a school must
have both for children's safety and to ensure harmonious social
life, and it would seem important for children to be given the
justifications for these rules. Some of these may be rather complex and difficult for children to understand in all their subtlety,
but the attempt should be made. At least children are then
learning that there are rational reasons for rules, and that they
need not be simply a matter of adult whim. It is even more
desirable to help children to derive the rules themselves from
principles on a simple concrete level which they can understand,
rather than vice versa, and there are many situations in school
where this is a possibility. A discussion with children about
appropriate behaviour and organization for a story, where they

can think out the need for behaving so that everybody can hear and see the teacher, will help them to derive rules about being quiet and not sitting in a way that obscures the view of children sitting behind them.

> A teacher of a class of six-year-olds found that the children had some difficulty in remembering to put their chairs on their tables before they left in the afternoon, and she was irritated that she constantly had to remind them to do this. Finally she asked them why they thought this was done. After considerable thought they came to the conclusion themselves that it was to ease the job of the cleaner in sweeping the floor, and having understood the rule they found it easier to keep.

A discussion about clearing up can help children to understand the need for co-operation and fairness in sharing chores and to derive rules to ensure both. The same principle holds good for individual children.

> A six-year-old left a class book he had been reading open on a desk and then began to paint, with the result that the book got splashed. The teacher asked him what he thought would happen to the book when he went into the next class. After a little thought he said it would be used by the new children in the class, and without further prompting added that he should have put it away before beginning to paint.

There will inevitably be occasions when children behave in ways that are socially and ethically undesirable either by flouting the rules or through not understanding them, and in these situations teachers have to intervene to help settle disputes, to redirect behaviour and perhaps to reprimand. But it is equally if not more important that socially and ethically desirable behaviour is acknowledged and shown to be valued by teachers. Moral development consists in learning what ought to be done as well as what ought not to be done, and it is partly by having desirable behaviour acknowledged and valued, and where possible the reason given for valuing such behaviour, that this learning takes place.

It has been suggested that a moral value system is crucial to a mature morality, and it therefore seems important to define the concept of 'value'. Values are an organized system for perceiving and interpreting situations and for determining behaviour. They are established as a child evaluates behaviour and makes autonomous decisions about the best ways of behaving. Gradually his evaluations begin to have some consistency; faced with the same alternatives on several occasions, his choice of behaviour becomes the same because he has given worth to that behaviour. His evaluating thus leads to valuing. The notion of choice which is thus built into the concept of 'value' is important for two reasons.

Firstly, making choices in valuing is an individual and autonomous affair. We cannot really speak of choice if the selection was not autonomous but the result of coercion of some sort. This is yet another reason why it is important for children to have opportunities for social interaction with their peers, where they are in a position to explore alternative ways of behaving free of adult constraint.

Secondly, evaluating one way of behaving as against another implies that children should be exposed to appropriate models of behaviour. Psychological evidence indicates that parental models have a crucial influence on moral development, and sociological evidence suggests that cultural and subcultural differences frequently determine the nature of parental models. The good examples that teachers can set in their own behaviour to children constitute important models of behaviour which children can evaluate, and where a child has a parental model which is over-aggressive, punitive or ethically undesirable in some way, these examples provide important alternative models.

> In one five-year-old class, where there was a boy whose behaviour was somewhat bizarre and unpredictable, the teacher's understanding and tolerance of his difficulties was reflected in the reactions of the other children to him. They looked after him, saw that he was in the right place at the right time, helped him to dress and undress, fetched him his dinner and so on, treating him with the gentleness and thoughtfulness which the teacher displayed.

Teachers inevitably present models of behaviour in all their dealings with individual children, with the class as a whole, with their colleagues and with parents; it is not only their conscious attempts to behave in certain ways themselves and to evaluate children's behaviour in certain ways, but also words and actions of which they are not consciously aware, which influence children. Moreover, it is often impossible to predict what words and what aspects of behaviour children will pay attention to and what will influence them. The ethical area is probably one in which there is a great deal of incidental learning, and it is important that teachers should be conscious of the kinds of models they present for children's learning. To quote Williams [52], 'The child does not consciously decide to select a particular adult as a model. We are furthering or hindering a child's moral progress every time we foster his self-respect by giving real responsibility, or remain uninterested in trivial problems that loom large to him, or make arbitrary decisions overriding his developing ability to think for himself. We are all moral educators, whether we like it or not.'

The poetry and stories, both fictional and non-fictional, which teachers present to children also provide models, since they are concerned, at however simple a level, with relationships and sometimes with certain moral issues. The same principles apply to these models as to those presented by teachers in their own behaviour; it is impossible to predict what aspects children will select to pay attention to, and it is therefore important for teachers to be aware of the moral issues involved. These values are particularly significant where they may have a cumulative effect through the frequency with which they appear in the stories commonly presented to children. The 'romantic myth', that physical beauty always goes with 'goodness' and ugliness with 'badness', that passive beauty always wins the best prizes, and that the major reward for possessors of this attribute is to live 'happily ever after' without further effort, is a value that permeates many of the fairy stories commonly told to children. As Bantock [3] suggests, it would also seem important to scrutinize closely the values to which children are exposed outside school, through the mass media and in popular culture. Only after such a scrutiny has taken place can teachers become aware of the extent to which they are reinforcing these values or presenting alternative ones, decide on the extent to which they wish to do either, and consider ways in which they can help children to become more discriminating in evaluating these models.

A mature morality has been defined as involving moral principles, which provide justifications for behaving in certain ways, as well as values. While valuing is a personal affair, values come to be part of a cultural consensus as they are integrated with principles. It would therefore seem important to help children to reflect on experiences involving moral issues. Reflection is essential in educating children toward understanding of principles. The following conversation between an eight-year-old boy and his teacher took place during a school sports day:

Boy: 'I'm going to hit Graham J.'
Teacher: 'Why?'
Boy: 'Because he tripped me up in the relay.'
Teacher: 'Did he do it on purpose?'
Boy: 'I am not sure.'
Teacher: 'Will that make a difference?'
Boy: 'Yes, it would if I was sure.'
Teacher: 'What are you going to do then?'
Boy: 'Perhaps I had better forget it in case it was an accident.'

In this situation the teacher helped the boy to a maturer level of behaviour and understanding by provoking him to reflect on motives. Younger children will naturally find this more difficult, but still the attempt should be made. A teacher of a class of five-year-old children entered the classroom to find that a battle between two boys had resulted in one boy's jacket being torn. The boy responsible for this protested that the other boy had 'started it'. She asked what sort of reaction might be expected from the mother of the boy with the torn jacket. He agreed that the mother would be angry, but, still unrepentant, repeated that the other child had started the fight. Although on this occasion the teacher had been unable to get the boy to re-evaluate his behaviour, at least she had been successful in making him aware of the consequences.

The fact that moral development involves caring and valuing as well as principles implies that moral development is related to emotional as well as to intellectual development. The relationship between emotional and moral development is a complex one. On the one hand, since moral issues involve interpersonal relationships, the education of the emotions is a vital aspect of moral education. As has already been suggested, moral behaviour involves insight into and sensitivity toward other people's feelings, motives and experiences, and caring about these. On the other hand, the emotional dependence of young pre-school children on their parents is a powerful force causing children to identify with parents and determining the acquisition of many parental values and attitudes. This identification results in children incorporating into themselves certain of what they perceive to be the attitudes and values of parents so that they become a source of inner control of behaviour. This process of internalizing certain aspects of parent's judgments and behaviour Freud calls introjection, and the resulting internal system of controls he calls the super-ego. The super-ego has been equated with conscience, but it is a very primitive form of conscience, for, unlike the conscious moral controls that arise from mature reflection and sensitivity, the super-ego is unconscious. What the individual is aware of are the feelings of guilt and fear he experiences when he transgresses the demands of the super-ego, not the sources of these which originate in early childhood. The super-ego is thus in some measure irrational. For example, a woman, now middle-aged, was brought up in a home where it was regarded as sinful to go to the cinema on Sundays. She herself no longer regards this as sinful and sometimes does go to the cinema on Sundays, but she still experiences some feeling of guilt when she does so. It is significant that she experiences no such feelings when she watches a film on television on a Sunday (there was no television in her childhood). The super-ego exists alongside a rational morality, and the mature adult may need to subject many of these primitive feelings to reflection and a logical reappraisal.

The function of teachers in this area is to help children develop in ways that lead ultimately to a mature, rational morality. Perhaps the subtle interdependence between the education of the emotions and reason, makes this one of the most complex as it is surely one of the most important tasks a teacher has.

CHAPTER 9

Psychological Standpoint

EDUCATION is a multi-disciplinary subject. To get some idea of its complexity one needs only to take a look at a college of education syllabus to see all that is involved academically of psychology, philosophy, sociology, history of education, comparative education plus a large range of arts and sciences, and an equally attentive look at a class of forty young children to see what is involved practically. It can hardly be expected that primary school teachers should have full knowledge of all subjects, and yet they must have some fundamental knowledge of each, for the task of teaching involves not only knowing about the intellectual, physical, social and emotional growth and development of children, but also about the subject matter that children are to learn.

By some means a teacher has to unify these different aspects of knowledge into a framework that structures his/her professional activities. Underlying this framework will be the beliefs and values the teacher holds both consciously and unconsciously; these will provide the bases for all assumptions made about what he is doing. Beliefs about education are many and varied, and knowledge about education (in the sense of what has been scientifically verified) is small. It is therefore possible in our country, which enjoys a great deal of teacher freedom, to go into classrooms where the aims, content and procedures of education are very different. The writers of this book share some common assumptions about learning and teaching and, in the belief that all teachers should try to isolate and examine their professional ideas, they decided that the fundamentals of their own psychological viewpoint as revealed in the various chapters should be stated. This in no sense claims to be a comprehensive or complete account of any psychological theory.

The following are generalizations from psychological knowledge and professional experience which the present writers affirm:

1. Children are unique persons and their individuality is to be acknowledged and respected.
2. Each person constructs his own mind as a result of interaction with things and people in his environment, and interaction between his own inner experiences.
3. Learning is continuous and knowledge cumulative.
4. The concept of 'stages' in intellectual development is useful in helping to understand some distinguishable phases of development in a child's thought.
5. Children encouraged in co-operative efforts with other children and with teachers will collaborate in the search for and the sharing of knowledge.
6. The mental processes involved in the search for knowledge and understanding contain their own self-expanding and extending propulsion.

It seems important to focus on individual differences and 'personal uniqueness' because the job of teaching in the practical situation would seem on the surface to deny the possibility of treating each child as unique. Classes are large and traditional practices lead to the acceptance of class or group instruction as the only way to deal with numbers of children. There is so much to be taught, that selecting, ordering and presenting subject matter can absorb all the time a teacher can spare. If one then extends the concept of teaching to include its relationship to what is learned by each individual, then an equal amount of attention needs to be given to the quality of understanding, the nature of error and the degree of interest the learner is giving to the subject matter. This makes teaching a complex task; it can never be simple though skill and experience may help to simplify it.

Whatever techniques teachers employ they know they are concerned with individual persons and are constantly reminded by children that this is so, sometimes pleasantly by the speed, originality and spontaneity of learning one child or another shows, sometimes not so pleasantly in the reactions of difficult behaviour such as sullenness, aggressiveness or indifference. But it must be acknowledged that some academic psychologists (in contrast to those working in fields of applied psychology, e.g. educational and clinical psychologists) differ from teachers on this count. Academic psychologists, as scientists, search for general principles and attempt to formulate laws about the behaviour of large numbers of people. To do this they sometimes have to ignore inner feelings and ideational states of persons which are infinitely variable and difficult to measure with the degree of objectivity and rigour demanded by scientific method.

There are many theories and schools of psychology. Teachers have a bewildering array to choose from. The writers of this book have found their educational values best served by psychologies which assume that a person's inner experience has a reality which must be acknowledged, in addition to his externally observable behaviour, in any descriptive or explanatory account of his life. We contend that when we teach we need to be aware of the fact that the patterns of reaction that each child displays to persons, things and situations are the result of his own continuous cumulative growth and development, and that his individual history of personal experience is recorded and categorized in active mental patterns that are ready for further experience.

We look to psychology for an account of the development of persons which identifies the psychological processes and structures they have in common and the factors that influence and shape their progress. We have found the works of Jean Piaget, Jerome Bruner, Susan and Nathan Isaacs particularly helpful by their presentation of a coherent account of how children construct their minds, and the part adults play in the process. Many psychologists in Europe and the U.S.A. are amplifying, clarifying and refining this genetic-psychological approach to child development, providing further research evidence to support its use as a framework to relate to educational practice. The following is a summary of some of its ideas which have been used and illustrated in preceding chapters.

A new-born baby is psychologically reactive to his environment. We can observe his bodily responses to the various kinds of stimuli that he encounters in being bathed, dressed, fed, cradled, etc. and if we assume that he is at first psychologically neutral, it is soon obvious that as things happen to him in being cared for he is spontaneously reactive to them; as each happening impinges on the neutrality some stimuli are actively sought again (Chapter 2). His own active responses and the experienced results of those actions constitute a baby's basic way of getting to 'know' the world around him. Each kind of action and its accompanying feelings, by constant use, builds up an inner mental schema, i.e. an organization constructed within the individual which is partly derived from experience of the action and partly from the attributes of the object acted upon. For example, a grasping action applied to a piece of blanket will give a baby experience of his own movement and feelings, and sensory information about the woollen object in the external world.

This schema-building process starts off at or soon after birth and, beginning with innate reflex responses, e.g. grasping, sucking, looking, etc. extends to cover a whole range of acquired sensory-motor actions associated with the senses and movement response itself. The schema building process has two aspects: assimilation and accommodation, both essential for further growth. A baby actively stretches out and treats everything as an object of his activity: he tries to incorporate or absorb things to these activities (in early months everything seems to be a 'suckable'). This is assimilation, but not all objects are amenable to the actions he has to perform; things roll away, drop out of sight, move unexpectedly or stay put and give rise to resistance and sometimes hurtful feelings. Experiences which the actions bring vary and these differences require some adaptation on the part of the child if he is to change or diversify his action schemata, i.e. 'accommodate' to the new experiences and bring about new patterns of action to be tried out, practised and further modified. These action schemata extend themselves by use and it is the 'accommodation' aspect that brings about the increasing diversity of action and reaction that babies display during the first two years of life. As each phase of physical growth brings increasing motor skills such as sitting up, crawling, standing and walking, the active schemata are further applied to an ever-increasing range of objects in widening dimensions of space.

Indeed, by the age of two, a child recognizes a great number of objects and persons which are to him persistent and recurring: he has some knowledge of the extension of space and finds things high, low, behind, under: he knows some constant patterns of happenings connected with results he can bring about by his own action, and he recognizes some which other people bring about by their actions. This means that his schemata have a power of anticipation so that he can co-ordinate his perceptions and actions and try out the results to test their correctness, finding out which anticipations can be relied on and which must be changed.

It is thought that the emergence of two processes, play and imitation, which can clearly be observed in a child's range of activities in his second year of life are differentiations made within the general adaptive developments of sensory-motor activity. One of the important differences between human beings and other living creatures is their superiority in plasticity of action. The schemata, which are dynamic organizations, can be multiplied in excess of the moment to moment adaptation of a child. Some are strengthened and refined by constant active use in interaction with the environment: some are formed to meet a particular event and disappear: others would disappear for want of stimulation if the emergence of play did not prevent this. In play a child takes up the assimilating aspect of the schemata and exercises it according to his own wishes. At first this is likely to be mere repetition of the schema usually accompanied by enjoyment (e.g. babbling of a baby—see chapter on music) but later, objects, or toys as we call them, are brought in to further this activity when deliberate make-believe play becomes a definite possibility.

A young child's constant repetition of his own actions extends to the attempt to repeat the actions of other people. This then involves him in constant accommodation to get his activity matched to theirs. These accommodative efforts give rise to inner (mental) representations of what has been imitated. Such representations are images and they are our nearest inner match to the outer world which we know by common perception (see Chapter 3). Because the preferred sense of most people is vision, it is commonly assumed that the word 'image' refers only to a visual picture in one's mind, but psychologists

point out that auditory, tactile, olfactory, gustatory, kinaes-
thetic and haptic images also are formed. Although some people
produce and use one mode more strongly than another, most
people form images in all modes and use them in complex
ways which we never stop to analyse. It is important for adults
to remind themselves that young children must construct these
internal symbols in the course of their lives, and that we can
assist this process by providing opportunity for varied sensory
impression, expression and appreciation of the different imagal
modes (art). We can hinder children's development by ignoring
or denying the importance of this internal process.

The development of speech in the third year brings about a
rapid extension in a child's activities. As he grasps the vocabulary and sentence forms of his culture, he has a new tool for
extending his knowledge and memory by drawing on that of
other people, where previously he had to rely solely on his own
searching activities which were limited to his immediate
environment. Language is another symbolic process; like
imagery, in that it stands for or represents things in the world
by naming them, unlike imagery, in that it in no way matches
those things but is an arbitrary cultural sign for them. It is also
different in that it can stand for those internal experiences as
well, for we name and discuss images, dreams, wishes, feelings
and ideas.

At first, a child uses words for identification and description
of those things he notices or wants, but by the fourth year
'what's that' is followed by other question forms beginning
with 'where', 'when' and 'how', eventually leading to the
important word 'why' which, in the range of explanations it
brings from adults, is an entry into the heritage of human
knowledge and the means for adding to it. If there is expansion
in vocabulary and development in sentence structure during
this period, the foundations of key concepts, as used by adults,
are laid down. By these we mean certain vast, all-embracing
ideas which structure, relate and cohere a person's experiences
past, present and intended. The preceding chapters have
referred to 'key' concepts of time, space, number, causality
and classification in various ways, and have shown how the
foundations for future subject learning are laid in these pre-
school years.

Parents and nursery school teachers know this period in a child's development well, it brings such talkativeness and demands for attention with its intensive 'whys', driving adults back and back on their own explanations, sometimes to the point of exasperation. It is during this time that children learn more ideas about the possible causes of events, reasons for human behaviour and ways of classifying objects and experiences.

However, it is also a time which brings confusion in a child's mind, for words sometimes refer to things he has not perceived before or understood as adults intend. He struggles to give meaning to all that he hears but, because of his limited experience, is bound to bring some wrong and hazy ideas to the fore. As long as our words refer to fairly commonly perceived phenomena we know that these will easily be understood by others, but when we get on to some of the relations we have constructed to make further meaning out of our experience (e.g. logical, causal, spatial, numerical, moral relations), then it is more difficult to convey to others what we refer to. That is why young children, when questioned on number, moral or aesthetic ideas, seem to give such amusing or silly answers, for we can too often assume a word we have used is having the same meaning for them as for us. It has been shown in this book how important it is to pay attention to the understanding of words that refer to concepts or categories not abstracted from immediate experience, but abstracted from ideas about that experience (see Chapters 6, 7, 8).

Much has been written about language and thought and the relationship between the two. It is necessary for teachers to keep in mind the development of both as separate, but not discrete, aspects of mental functioning. We endeavour to find out from young children, by observation and discussion, what meanings they are giving to words, and we help them to develop, refine and clarify these. Sometimes, further active experience is required to make sense of a new idea: sometimes new words or a new combination of words enable him to gain insight. All the chapters in this book concentrate on the importance of first-hand experience for young children. This has been to emphasize our belief that learning takes place in a total context of immediate action, feeling and perception. From such a total experience some new aspect is selected and added to past knowledge. But this does not mean that we ignore the impact on children of information about things past, places distant and innovations of modern technology. Children hear words about things they do not know and ask us questions. Although the information we may have to give is too difficult to be fully understood by a child, by talking with him we can convey that there are facts, explanations and justifications to come, thus providing some preparatory schemata ready to be filled out and connected as more experience and later learning take place.

To focus on one aspect, either thought or language, at the expense of the other can lead to shallow thinking marked by apparent verbal facility, or to the frustrations, aggressiveness or withdrawal of inarticulateness. Children need constant encouragement to express their thoughts in words and other media and to submit these to the tests of logic, science and the judgments of others: the known means of transforming personal ideas into knowledge, i.e. ideas which are thus held in common.

The stage of development in which children attend to and act upon what is immediately perceived by them has been referred to as 'pre-operational'; the sensory-motor and intuitive substages come under this heading. The chapters on mathematics, science, music and movement have mentioned in particular the sensory-motor stage in which first-level ideas of a world of permanent objects (separate from what a baby can *do* to them) emerge. The chapters on art, music and literature have referred to the intuitive stage when children learn to represent their own inner experiences through the medium of symbols (images and words). Both substages have shown how much depends on perception and remembering: it is what a child observes in the here and now that he notes, repeats and acts on. The continuity of time for him is his own sequence of experience which he is beginning to build up into more or less stable ideas; space is the appearance of things in relation to position and distance from himself; things are classified by their perceptible attributes or their use. The words 'egocentric' and 'irreversible' have been used in connection with these stages to show a child's main dependence on his own point of view, both in relation to objects (see chapter 6) and the motives of other people (see Chapter 8).

The move into concrete-operational thought marks a new stage in development. It brings about de-centering in a child's mental activities. He learns to be able to see objects and people in relation to each other and separate from his own feelings, wishes and perceptions. He builds up permanent ideas of conservation concerning number, time, space, weight, volume, cause, and learns to use more complex classificatory systems and logical operations. He learns to reflect (to stop and *think*) on his own actions and relate these mentally to his perceptions so that he is carrying out internally (in thought) ideas which previously could only persist if acted out (see Chapter 6).

Teachers in the first school will be concerned particularly with growth within the intuitive stage and the moves into concrete operational thinking. We have shown that children continue to need the support of present, or very recently experienced, perceptual material to assist them in making new connections between previously organized ideas, hence our insistence on the provision of well-stocked classrooms and frequent visits to places outside school. We have also shown that the move from perceptually based ideas to conceptual thought is a long slow process, as concepts have to be constructed in relation to each area of subject matter. For instance, knowledge of time is not learned in mathematics lessons only, it is a highly abstract concept that is formed from many abstractions made at different mental levels in a variety of contexts. In school these would be contexts of scientific experimentation, dance and movement, artistic representation, music-making and literary imagining. Each subject is structured within some key concepts and values, but it also has its own particular concepts, values and terminology. To appreciate the existence of subject areas, their similarities and differences, is an adult activity, but that is what children are working towards and their first efforts should be marked by clarity and confidence. Chapter 10 describes a class of children organized in a way that encouraged individual interests in a social setting; there were no timetabled class lessons in particular subjects, but the examples show that the children were learning science, mathematics, music, etc.

It would be misleading to give the impression that we believe the self-extending processes involved in the cycle of experiencing, expressing, testing, judging and reasoning develop and function in isolation. They emerge and continue this function in a social context. The preceding chapters have stressed and illustrated the contribution of adults in general and the role of teachers in particular to every child's growth and development. Special mention is made of interaction with peers, not only because human warmth is engendered by sharing activities but also because intellectual stimulation is created. No matter how tolerant, considerate or permissive adults are, children do not possess equal rights with them. The framework of home life is constructed primarily to serve adult purposes and, however a child is reared, he has to learn to adapt to the circumstances that prevail. However, in school, where there are numbers of children at the same levels of age and of experience, they have more scope to exercise overtly the demands for equal rights. Parents and teachers often voice the opinion that nursery school or play group experience is valuable because it provides opportunities for children to learn to share things with other children. It is not always clear what they hope children will gain from this. It could be that they want to see 'nice, socially-conforming' behaviour with an absence of the physical violence children can show if thwarted. But, as the chapter on moral development shows, this can mean many things for a child. He may conform socially by behaving as expected only when the adult is looking; he may withdraw his own claims and retreat from the over-assertiveness of others, or he may choose to flaunt the authority of adults. We have tried to show that children indeed must share, and that the sharing of opinions, ideas and feelings is as important as sharing possessions. The shared experiences of the music, art and literature of other children at a similar level of creative expression can be the beginning of understanding of great art, music and literature in human history: the challenge of other children's questions and comments on his discoveries in work and play can be the beginning of appreciation of criticism. The pleasure of sharing is often acknowledged, and indeed it usually involves emotional satisfaction, but it also involves intellectual extension and we have tried to give emphasis to the latter because the progress of human knowledge depends on it. We believe that children should be introduced to this idea by deliberate and continual encouragement of varied group activities and discussion. We consider that in fostering the attitude of co-operation rather than competition the continued progress of each individual and the group is ensured.

The problem of 'motivation' in human learning is a complex one and there is much current work to be read on the subject for those who seek enlightenment. The present writers have adopted the point of view that whatever its source, the spontaneity, strength and tenacity of young children's power to learn in the first two years of life is such that it is worth fostering and encouraging. This means allowing for continued self-selection of activity and the acceptance of 'errors' as information by which one can correct one's practice or ideas rather than behaviour to be eliminated. Children can soon pick up the use of extrinsic motives in learning such as 'pleasing the adult' or 'finding out what the teacher wants'. While we would not deny the supporting and bridging function of these motives for children as they try to master a new skill or idea, we need to be aware of the temporary nature we wish to assign to them, so that they are not used to the extent that children become deflected from using intrinsic searching-to-know schemas.

The chapter on moral development has referred to the work of psychoanalytic psychology which has defined some of the mechanisms involved in these deflections of inner mental growth which may separate in a person some aspects of his early purposes and strivings and make it difficult for him to achieve an integrated personality in adult life. The complexity of the inner life with its areas of fantasy and confusion is part of our human condition; education can lead to clarification and understanding if teaching is seen as supporting, extending and continuing purposes from within. We never know exactly what is going on in another person, we have to assume or infer that he feels and strives and wishes and suffers as we do. We can provide children with conditions for experience and we can offer possible ways of structuring thoughts and ordering values, but in the last analysis we cannot *give* them experience itself: they select it and each one has his own.

When key concepts were referred to no specific mention was made to the concept of 'self', that emerging unifying idea that slowly gathers cohesion throughout childhood as a person reflects upon his experiences. When we want to talk to each other about the feelings and ideas we have we say' *I* feel . . .' or '*I* think . . .' and refer to a 'self' or uniting principle within us as a reality as convincing as that of the world around us. This inner reality is difficult to describe: ideas about our reliance on the permanence of our memories, images, perceptions and thoughts seldom rise into full conscious awareness. Underlying the educative work described in the previous chapters is the assumption that if children are helped to become consciously aware not only of what they are learning but also of how they are learning and what can be done with that knowledge, then, later by adolescence they will have formed 'self' concepts which will enable them to use the many aspects of themselves with enjoyment and skill in pursuit of individual and social ideals.

CHAPTER 10

Teachers and Children

WE HAVE considered briefly the underlying principles which we believe should guide us in planning children's first years in school particularly in relation to the foundations of their mental life and the cultivation of the early stages of those thinking abilities on which they must rely for the rest of their lives. It is not possible to draw all these threads together in the description of one classroom which follows. But this book is intended for those who have worked, or are working, with young children and for them a pattern may emerge in outline which they themselves can fill in with their own thought and experience.

My intention was to observe without participation because I wanted the observation to be as objective as possible, within the limits of the conditions, i.e. that in choosing a particular school at all one's point of view about the value of what is happening is immediately declared. One's interest, too, is declared by what one considers noteworthy. The description of what was actually done or said can, however, be accurate though never, of course, complete. What I describe was only a fraction of all that was going on and even the whole would not have covered the range of experience of a week or a term.

It proved even more difficult than I had supposed to remain passive in the company of children who made the immediate assumption that any adult in the room was bound to be at their service, but, unless directly applied to, I gave neither help nor apparent interest.

The scene is set in a new estate still in the process of construction, which from one angle seems to consist of the systematic destruction of a country area. Each term blocks a view of suburban fields from another classroom and substitutes instead uninspired cliffs of flats with only too clearly built-in obsolescence. The way to school is muddy and the landscape is littered with the machinery and the noise of destruction and construction. The usual incoherence and disorganization of the building industry is displayed: there are new classrooms which cannot be used because the staircase has not been built to the right specifications and there has been misunderstanding about what was to be provided. There is the sheer fatigue of bearing the noise and the dirt and the disruption of careful planning because of the increase in numbers without increased accommodation. The story is almost a standard one and is only mentioned to prevent any thought arising that the school to be described is in any way in a favoured position.

The children fall into the 'average' class: they are neither rich nor, with a few exceptions, extremely poor. They are mostly well nourished, adequately clothed and looked after. As my car crawled along the unmade road full of mothers and children and prams and babies, viewing the entry to school from behind, I was struck, not for the first time, with the efforts made by young parents to get themselves and their children clothed, fed and delivered at school by around 8.45 a.m. There is more than effort involved, there is a certain solemnity about the ritual of parting. These children enjoy school but for young children the parting each morning is never, perhaps, without its pangs. It is a wise school that allows for a gradual and informal beginning to the day. On this morning almost as many parents as children came into the school: some to see the teachers, some to help their children undress, some to see some treasured 'creation' of the day before and yet others to see the chicks whose hatching had been a central drama of many days for the children. Parent–teacher co-operation can take many forms and in the infants' school there are many opportunities for this informal knitting together of home and school which young children still wish for and need. Independence is of slow growth: school must give opportunities for this gradual weaning. There are needs for one's own life away from home and for separated, personal areas of experience and these will differ from child to child both according to his particular circumstances and to his nature, but they cannot be satisfied by artificially imposed separation at a certain age. They must be viewed, as all else, developmentally and seen as part of a whole pattern of growth. There are, in this school as in all others, children for whom school is a refuge, whose homes cannot easily be connected with the school, but for most children the joining at this stage can be easy and can vary according to need. The biggest stumbling block to this is that it makes very heavy demands on a teacher of over forty children with eighty (or more!) parents. In this school, the 'vertical grouping' organization means a longer association with the children and a building up of knowledge about families whose children normally enter the same classes as older brothers and sisters. As in all schools, the head teacher here has to be the clearing house for many family problems, but the easy access to the individual teacher, which is encouraged, tackles some problems at source and prevents many others arising. A parent who can just 'have a word' about a disturbed night or an upset can help a teacher to understand a child's behaviour and help her to know whether a quiet withdrawal or a distraction is to be encouraged. In the particular classroom I was joining there was an area arranged like a sitting room with one battered 'easy' chair with cushions and rugs on the floor. This was used both as the gathering place for stories and singing or listening to music, and for those who wanted quietness to read or think. 'The chair' was often used as a refuge: I noticed that one child, who had lost the struggle for a piece of equipment already in use by another, went straight to the chair and rested his head on the cushion for a few minutes of comfort and thought and then cheerfully turned to another employment.

The children were manifestly 'self-employed'. When they first came into the room each child made for some activity and most children very rapidly completed some piece of creative work. (The need for a fully prepared, well-equipped room is obvious. Waiting about for materials or insufficient choice or number of materials takes the edge off the children's power to concentrate which is one of the most important abilities we are trying to develop.)

There were many interesting rhythms to be perceived: this initial attack seems to be natural to most children unless they are ill or sad. As this died down there seemed to be a turning towards the teacher for her contribution. The children gathered together a few at a time and joined the teacher who was by now seated in the sitting area with her guitar at her side. There were looks of pleased anticipation for the expected story and discussion and music. There is a continuing dialogue in this room between teacher and individual, teacher and class, child and child which it is very difficult to analyse though it can be described. These children are busy educating themselves and each other, taking sustenance from the teacher and from books when their own resources give out. A selection of examples will illustrate these points.

> Two boys of 6 and 7
> 7-year-old: 'My brother likes that tune.'
> 6-year-old: 'How old's your brother?'
> 7-year-old: 'Nine.'
> 6-year-old: 'Is he in the Juniors?'
> 7-year-old: 'Well, where d'you think he'd be?'

> Girl of six to me:
> 'My nanny's coming to see me tonight. (pause) Have you got a nanny?' (Then, as if contradicting herself) 'Oh no, of course not!—You're one yourself, aren't you?'

(Incidentally the conversation that starts with an apparently irrelevant remark such as the foregoing has usually a significance for the child. On enquiry, I found that this child's parents were on the point of separating and the grandmother was the stable element in her life and would probably take her to live with her. This was clearly very near the surface of her mind and was very likely the reason why she came to speak to me at all.) This examination of one's own thought is an important ingredient of intellectual growth.

> One Pakistani boy announced that he had been born in England. Much later in the morning another boy said thoughtfully to the teacher: 'I thought all boys born in England had white skins. But they can't have.'

These conversations reflect the teacher's objective attitude in promoting thinking. It is, of course, no mere 'reflection', but rather a habit of mind which has been extended to the children. Such an attitude contains little overt personal judgment: it consists largely of the presentation of ideas for scrutiny. Nevertheless the selection of ideas for presentation implies and reflects the teacher's own values (see Chapter 8).

> Boy (5.0 holding a large magnifying glass between himself and me. 'You've got two noses.' (pause) 'You've got two glasses— two *pairs* of glasses—four glasses! You've got two mouths' (moving away the magnifying glass) 'now you've got half a pair of mouths', etc., etc. He seemed to be talking himself into understanding, doing spontaneously the practice which many people believe will only take place when insisted on or time-tabled.

There were many such instances of practice.

> A boy of five was playing with a large set of nesting boxes. He returned them to the large box on a trial and error system, with, indeed, many errors. As soon as they were in, he took them out again and continued activity with them until he could pack them in swiftly without error. He made no attempt at ranging them in order *before* packing though of course his task would have been made easier if he had, but after the job was mastered, he set them out in order and seemed to be contemplating them. Then once more he rapidly assembled them and turned to something else.

> A boy of six was determined to get a note from a bugle and practised for over fifteen minutes without success. He tried again the next day and discovered the technique. He returned at intervals to this fatiguing task until he could feel satisfied that he could produce a note at will.

This urge to learn seems to be present in every young child and nothing could be more important in the long run than to find the means to retain it. The point to note here is that self-undertaken practice needs no artificial motivation. It is clearly seen to be tied to a present need and the outcome too is equally clear. The importance of the contemporary nature of effective practice is sometimes overlooked. 'You'll be sorry you can't read when you're grown up' refers to a possibility too distant in time to provide a genuine motive for a child. The concept of 'reinforcement repetition' is not an adequate one to cover human learning. Practice, as these children undertake it, is a kind of recording and pinning down of an experience or an achievement at a more conscious level, leading to an organization of what they know into functional units which, in their turn, lead to new achievements.

> When I sat down in as secluded a place as I could find a girl of six said, 'What are you doing? Writing? Well, I'll sit next to you. I am going to work too.'

It would seem from such a remark that one could perceive the beginnings of an idea of 'work', involving *conscious* intent, effort and application as distinct from 'play' where the effort may be as great but the purposes less clearly in the conscious mind.

> A seven-year-old was reading dramatically but quietly to two five-year-olds, and all was peace in the corner. Two six-year-olds, both non-readers were looking at a book which contained lists of Christian names. David had found his but Sally could not find hers. 'You're looking in the wrong list', said David. 'How do you know?' 'Because my name is in it and I am a boy.' They shifted their attention to the other list. 'Sally' was not on it. 'Could you write it in?' I wrote it lightly in pencil. 'I know why you did that. So that you could rub it out when I go to the Juniors!'

This provides another example of the verification of supposition mentioned earlier and elaborated in Chapter 2.

They then proceeded to find the names of their friends, matching them where necessary with names written on paintings, etc. No teaching of reading could have been more effective at this point or brought about the same involvement and concentration.

> Two children were playing a little question and answer game on a glockenspiel. They co-operated with quiet absorption as if they were in the room alone. When I next looked in their direction I discovered that each was playing his own tune independently on the same instrument. This was a great feat of concentration and involved much courteous waiting for the use of a particular note!

There were endless examples of categorizing.

> The teacher had brought a bag of stones from the beach and several children arranged and rearranged these in colours,

sizes and shapes. They dipped them in water and looked at their changing colours. One stone looked much darker in the water. 'I shall put it in with the dark stones.' 'You can't, because it gets dry again.' 'Well, I shall move it *then*.'

A girl of six with an unusual interest in cars was arranging pictures of cars into small, large, vans, lorries, etc. and was learning to read a great variety of words from labelled diagrams of the parts of a car she had found in a catalogue. Her own paintings of cars were many and various. I noticed that each contained as a rule only one feature apart from the outline, e.g. a steering wheel, petrol tank, etc. (It might be that a closer inspection of some of the drawings by children who are said to draw the same picture over and over again might reveal some such recording of detail and that for some children this 'listing' activity could be an important part of the organization of their thinking on a given theme.) The provision of a catalogue by the teacher to meet this child's interest was clearly bringing about further and more precise observation and vocabulary, for example, when another child referred to a picture of a 'shelter', she remarked 'it's a car port'.

Similar conversations were going on about shape and number. Leaves of seven or eight different shapes and greens had been compared and discussed with a small group and at intervals during the day several individual children could be seen arranging and rearranging these. The experience however was not a discrete one. One child smelt each one and then smelt a book and exclaimed in surprise, 'A book's got a smell too.'

This might lead to further work in many directions: the vocabulary of shape as well as the perception of shape, the ordered range of colour intensity and so on.

There were, as might be expected, innumerable paintings. These were not, in general, isolated 'works of art' but were part of the total experience the children were getting. All the paintings currently in the classroom were clearly expressing the children's views of various experiences and were not in the vague category of 'self-expression'. There were endless pictures of the chickens emerging from the eggs; one entitled 'It's wet at first'.

Many expressed various aspects of the human predicament as they saw it.

'The man is so busy watching a bird that he nearly fell under a car'.
'I am a fire engine. I wash the fire'.
Teacher: 'Wash it?'
'Wash it out, that means.'

Another picture reflected the way that children can find their own solutions or alleviations in symbolic play. A very insecure child in her first days at school drew a map to show the way home.

There was a reproduction of Turner's 'Fighting Temeraire' placed low on the wall where the children could really look into it. There had been much talk about this picture and it had noticeably influenced the children's observation of colour as shown in the richness and complexity of their pictures.

Other interesting objects were displayed which served both as material for aesthetic appreciation and as sources of conversation.

The builders had sliced some tree sections for them and the children had collected roots of different shapes and colours. A large tree root was being looked at.
Teacher: 'What does it take up to make it grow?' A thoughtful boy came out with:
'I know, it must take up leaves,'

and the talk that followed involved much thinking and comparison with, for instance, the acorn they had grown in a bottle.

There was much work with clay. The themes were never suggested by the teacher but she gave a good deal of incidental teaching of elementary techniques. 'You'd better put some more clay on that duck's neck, and smooth it off. You remember how the chicken's head fell off when it dried.' One child modelled a whale and asked for a label to be written: 'This is a whale. She is looking for some food for her babies and then she will go home.'
Small groups of children displayed and discussed their models, showing that absorbed interest in each other's work that children often display. The effort to explain, to demonstrate, and the to and fro between the teacher and the particular child and the other children furnished the most natural setting

for the real growth of language and understanding. In this connection it must be stressed that some current practice of artificial enrichment of language content by verbal *exercises* of one kind and another are likely to lead, at best, to a thin and superficial result because the language has not been acquired intrinsically and may well not be functional.

The teacher made little attempt to adjust her speech to 'the children's level'. She did, however, speak directly to each one of the children and often repeated the same idea in several ways. She used an adult vocabulary, with many semi-technical and precise terms, e.g., buckle, brace, amber, beige. In addition she used many abstract words like considerate, unobtrusive, thoughtful, some of which were taken up by the children and used experimentally as a means of understanding them.

> A child brushed past a desk and upset a box of pencils. Another child restored them all to the box and brought one to me that had lost its point. 'Was that considerate?' remarked a six-year-old girl.

> A boy (7.1) had been talking to the teacher about the goldfish and of its being 'alive' while some other things, for instance the stones, were dead. She gave him the words animate and inanimate. He was observed going round the classroom chanting:
> 'I'm animate but that's (table) inanimate.
> I'm animate but that's (flowers) animate.
> I'm animate but that's (window) inanimate.
> I'm animate but that wood—well it *was* a tree growing but now its inanimate.
> I'm animate but the guinea-pigs are—oh, they're animate too!'

It is worth noting that this principle of what might be called 'relevancy' was behind the provision of all kinds of material. For instance, the books displayed on the home-made screen were frequently changed during the term and were each put there for a purpose. A book about cameras, too difficult to read but full of good illustrations, was dipped into at intervals by a group of children playing with some discarded cameras. They called themselves 'press photographers' and very successfully imitated the curious dipping movements they had observed on T.V., and were also distinguishing items of 'news'. Their behaviour was somewhat more admirable than the adults they were imitating since they seemed to value achievements rather than disaster. They 'photographed' a huge model of a fire engine which had just been completed, a splendid picture by the child interested in cars, 'her best one yet', and 'snapped' a boy who had just learned to turn a somersault.

There were books about other current interests: fire engines, cars, flowers, unicorns and dinosaurs! After a time these were returned to the shelves to be rediscovered later. Almost every child read or looked at books some time in the day. Those who had reached a certain facility returned again and again for short bursts of deep concentration. All the seven-year-olds could read—not only *to* you but could read for themselves. They occasionally asked one for a word but many of them withdrew in silence for thirty minutes or more while they read through a book. (I tested their knowledge of what they had read and found them, indeed, 'reading for content'. Reading to the non-readers was their natural way of reading aloud.) A group of mixed ages is very reassuring to a young teacher relying on informal, self-undertaken learning. It is so much easier to *see* the progression than to have to take it on trust. When you see five- and six-year-olds apparently not making any marked advances for a day or two, or even a week or two, it is reassuring to look at the competent, knowledgeable and self-reliant seven-year-olds. This is particularly striking if you ask the seven-year-olds any specific questions about, for instance, number. They do not 'remember', they know.

Clusters of words were being assembled, embodying for instance, ideas of size.

One child had written and drawn a book about 'Things that are bigger than me.' There was much talk about size.
6-year-old: 'Who taught you that?'
Another 6-year-old: 'My sister.'
    'Which one?'
    'The big one, not Sandra, the very big one.'

Child (7) finding a picture of Big Ben.
    'Is there a little Ben?'
Child (7) A: 'I've drawn two fairies, one big and one little.'

Child (7) B: 'Are there really fairies?'
            A: 'No.'
            B: 'Then they can't be big and little.'

It was noteworthy that, during the two complete days of observation, no child behaved in a 'difficult' manner or had to be 'disciplined'. This is not to say that there were no 'incidents' which could have led to such behaviour, but each of these was used as a means of social growth and understanding instead.

A red-faced six-year-old pointed out another and said indignantly to the teacher: 'He hit me'. Teacher: 'I think you must have done something to him first, because you're looking cross and he isn't!' After a pause, while his agitation slowly evaporated, he said, with most objective candour, 'Well, I did!'

Again, only five out of the six skipping ropes came back after a period of play outside. Teacher: 'Well, the people who have been skipping had better go out and find the other one or somebody won't get a turn tomorrow!' The skipping rope was found.

The social awareness of the children was remarkable. One sad child had been listlessly leaning up against the teacher during the story and had remained leaning against the chair when she had gone. Another child, playing with some reins, peered at her and she hid her face. He leant down and said in a coaxing 'grown-up' voice, 'Shall I be your little horse?'

It was noticed in the apparatus sessions in the hall that each child seemed to enter with purpose and to go to a certain activity with a kind of passionate practising for a short time. Even during this solitary play, the children, unthinkingly it seemed, made way for each other and avoided clashes on the apparatus. As the period went on there were many little wordless, nameless, encounters when two children worked in rhythm together. These brief encounters sometimes led to more prolonged co-operation: two of the older children met on a horizontal ladder, took hands and walked alternately backward and forward: they then went together to the ropes and carried out a complicated piece of joint climbing and swinging with an appearance of high enjoyment. In their work in movement and on the apparatus the children were bold, inventive and relaxed. The 'practice' effort noted in many other areas was easy to observe. There were several common patterns: a number of attempts to achieve a certain feat, followed by success, followed by a triumphant repetition, by more routine repetitions, and finally by one or two somewhat perfunctory performances. Alternative sequences were observed: a number of trials with no success and a retreat to another activity or another piece of apparatus and a later returning to try again. One boy returned five times to a tricky feat without success. It was more common for children to attempt something which they could eventually achieve within the course of the period. Where no external pressures are put on children they seem to be able to judge what is within their capacity. The boy referred to was new to the school and inexperienced in this kind of work. This was an occasion when the teacher intervened and suggested some intermediate activity leading in the direction of what he was trying to achieve. It was felt that his desire to achieve this feat may have been due to a wish to emulate some other children of his age. If so, this was the only instance seen in the time of any competition with other children. The efforts made, and they were considerable, seemed to be solely directed towards improving their own performances.

The children's dance seemed very satisfying to them. It is difficult to describe because each child, for the most part, inhabited a world of his own. They moved freely around, sometimes with music, and, except for a few short lived 'duets', seemingly absorbed in thought and feeling in a way I can only describe as becoming more aware of themselves and more in control of themselves.

The children's activities in the classroom were too numerous for exhaustive mention. Many of them were continuing activities like reading, painting and so on which were taken up regularly where they had been left off. Others were small complete activities like the following: one child had read about making butter so a group collected cream from their milk and shook it indefatigably. They then took themselves off to the staffroom electric stove, made toast and spread on the butter and ate it. The value of a general 'helper' in primary schools was characteristically demonstrated in this activity. It was she who kept an eye on this while working quietly in a corner of the staffroom. She did not have to intervene but she gave the children (and the teacher!) confidence and security by her presence.

There are many views about keeping pets in the classroom and what pets to keep and there are surely few rules one can make about it. The part played by two stout and robust guinea-pigs in the lives of the children in this particular room was a very important one. They seemed particularly to play a role as comforters. Of course the animals' welfare must be safeguarded and each school comes to its own conclusions about how it can manage this aspect of the matter. It was noticeable that both with the chickens and the guinea-pigs much care was taken initially to explain the 'hold' and to demonstrate it. Those who 'got it right' quickly were only too ready to instruct others and seemed to take a natural responsibility for the animals' welfare.

They provided an endless source of interest and conversation.

> Boy, 6.9:   'She's female, not male.'
> Girl, 5.0:   'Are there two sorts?'
> Boy, 6.10: 'Of course—how could they have more without two sorts?'
> Girl, 5.0:   'What two sorts?'
> Boy, 6.10: 'Ladies and gentlemen—like us.'
> Girl, 7.0:   'She's a she guinea-pig, I looked underneath.'
> Girl, 5.0:   'How? I can't see!'
> Girl, 7.0:   'She's got things to feed babies on.'

Clearly, for some children, the relationship with the animal was also a kind of half-way house to social contact. This was true also of puppets. Two children used theirs rather as 'familiars'. One bride puppet was shown to me and the little girl remarked 'I sing with it'.

It may well be appropriate here to say a word or two about organization. With a class of over forty children in a room which would comfortably house twenty-five with all their equipment, organization can be of the utmost importance. To the question, Is there a framework to the day? the answer would be the same as that given by a modern mother when asked if she feeds her baby at regular times. A teacher observes the natural rhythm of her class and makes of it an unobtrusive framework or pattern of events which brings stability and security without regimentation. We make discoveries about divergent and convergent thinkers, yet in many schools we give no opportunity for the one or the other, losing, perhaps, part of the value of each. Some children, often the insecure ones, like to know the routine of the day, others need to cut across it. Each type of thinker almost certainly needs some of each, for obviously, these labels can only apply to the *overall* direction of their thinking, which leaves room for many areas where this does not apply.

The disposal of equipment, too, has its effects on the general security and harmonious behaviour of the class. In this class there were many ingenious arrangements: large vegetable racks for the storage of intractable 'odd materials' and lockers and shelves specially adapted to meet different storage problems. The reduction of even the legitimate noise from forty children is of importance; there were pieces of old carpet at strategic points, a thick table-cloth on the weighing table which reduced the clatter and rolling, etc. of the materials used: there was a relatively enclosed space made by the other equipment for musical instruments and even a 'closed season' for their use. Care and beauty in presentation, mounting, display and decoration bring a response in like terms. All these matters contribute to orderly behaviour and perhaps to orderly thinking.

Teachers of young children have developed much ingenuity in the collection of material of all kinds to provide stimulus and source material for their children. There is an enormous volume of 'odd' material to be found and many sources of supply of industrial waste. Every environment can supply vast quantities of natural objects animate and inanimate and the contents of junk shops and attics can supply numerous objects of historical interest as well as discarded electrical or mechanical equipment for investigation.

Many teachers have come to recognize the value of knowing something of the T.V. programmes the children watch and the comics they read. If we can refer to these in illustration or as shared enjoyment, we can help to knit the world together for the children and remove the sense that home and school are separate or even antagonistic.

We have tried to show throughout this book that the education of young children consists of the cumulative build-up of
'minute particulars' in which the attitudes formed and the
thinking abilities established are the most important elements.
The importance of the relationship between teachers and
children has been implicit in every chapter. A way of educating
based on developmental knowledge prescribes its own relationship of warm objectivity. Teachers and children must observe
the laws of good relationships and learn in the comparatively
sheltered environment of school what these are. No one would
attempt a formulation of rules but it is as certain that qualities of
integrity, respect, disinterestedness and generosity will lead to
good relationships as that arbitrariness, contempt, unkindness
and fear will lead away from them. The role of the adult in
the classroom is threefold: it is the role of a provider of material
and stimuli as well as of a 'climate' which allows for individual
and social growth, of a mediator of experience who looks on
every aspect of children's living as a means of learning and of a
teacher, whose professional knowledge and skill enables her to
teach at the moment of willingness and ability to learn.

The role of a teacher is a complex one and no stereotype will
fit it. Each teacher virtually builds his own role and there
should be scope for each to play his best part and for that part
to be, in itself, a developing one.

Select Bibliography

[1]   ALLPORT, G. W., *Pattern and Growth in Personality*, New York, Holt, Rinehart and Winston, 1963

[2]   BAILEY, E., *Discovering Music with Young Children*. Methuen, 1958

[3]   BANTOCK, G. H., *Education, Culture and the Emotions*, Faber, 1967

[4]   BARTLETT, SIR F., *Remembering*, Cambridge U.P., 1961

[5]   BLADES, J., *Orchestral Percussion Technique*, Oxford U.P., 1961

[6]   BLURTON-JONES, N. G., 'An Ethological Study of Some Aspects of Social Behaviour of Children in Nursery School', in D. Morris (ed.) *Primate Ethology*, Weidenfeld & Nicolson, 1967

[7]   BREARLEY, M. and HITCHFIELD, E., *A Teacher's Guide to Reading Piaget*, Routledge & Kegan Paul, 1966

[8]   BRONOWSKI, J., *Insight*, MacDonald & Co., 1964

[9]   BRUNER, J., *et al.*, *Studies in Cognitive Growth*, New York, Wiley, 1966

[10] BUTLER, R., *Creative Development*, Routledge & Kegan Paul, 1962

[11] CAWS, P., *The Philosophy of Science*, Princeton, Van Nostrand, 1965

[12] CLEGG, A. B. (ed.), *The Excitement of Writing*, Chatto & Windus, 1964

[13] DE CECCO, J. P., *The Psychology of Language, Thought and Instruction*, New York, Holt, Rinehart & Winston, 1968

[14] FORD, BORIS (ed.), *Young Writers, Young Readers*, Hutchinson, 1960

[15] FLAVEL, J. H., *The Developmental Psychology of Jean Piaget*, Princeton, Van Nostrand, 1963

[16] FROEBEL, FRIEDRICH, *The Education of Man*, D. Appleton & Co., 1888

[17] HOLLOWAY, G. E. T., *An Introduction to the Child's Conception of Space*, Routledge & Kegan Paul, 1967

[18] HOLLOWAY, G. E. T., *An Introduction to the Child's Conception of Geometry*, Routledge & Kegan Paul, 1967

[19]   HOLT, JOHN, *How Children Fail*, Pitman, 1967

[20]   HOLT, JOHN, *How Children Learn*, Pitman, 1968

[21]   HUNT, J. McV., *Intelligence and Experience*, New York, Ronald Press, 1961

[22]   ISAACS, NATHAN, 'Children's "Why" Questions', Appendix A *in* Isaacs, S.: *Intellectual Growth in Young Children*, Routledge & Kegan Paul, 1930

[23]   ISAACS, NATHAN, *New Light on Children's Ideas of Number*, Education Supply Association, 1960

[24]   ISAACS, SUSAN, *Intellectual Growth in Young Children*, Routledge & Kegan Paul, 1930

[25]   KAROLYI, O. *Introducing Music*, Harmondsworth, Penguin Books, 1965

[26]   LABAN, RUDOLF, *Modern Educational Dance*, 2nd ed., Macdonald & Evans, 1963

[27]   LABAN, RUDOLF and LAWRENCE, F. C., *Effort*, Macdonald & Evans, 1947

[28]   LANGER, S. *Problems of Art*, Routledge & Kegan Paul, 1957

[29]   LANGER, S., *Feeling and Form*, Routledge & Kegan Paul, 1959

[30]   LEWIS, M. M., *Language, Thought and Personality*, Harrap, 1963

[31]   LILLEY, IRENE M., *Friedrich Froebel, A Selection from his Writings*, Cambridge U.P., 1967

[32]   MEDAWAR, P. B. 'Scientific Method' in *The Listener*, 12th October, 1967

[33]   MILLAR, SUSANNA, *The Psychology of Play*, Harmondsworth, Penguin Books Ltd., 1968 (Pelican series)

[34]   NAVARRA, J. G., *The Growth of Scientific Concepts in the Young Child*, New York, Teachers College, Columbia University, 1955

[35]   NUFFIELD MATHEMATICS PROJECT, W. & R. Chambers & John Murray, 1968

[36]   OPIE, IONA and OPIE, PETER (ed.), *The Oxford Dictionary of Nursery Rhymes*, Oxford, Clarendon Press, 1951

[37]   PAYNTER, J. 'Learning from the Present' in *Music in Education*, 31/328, Novello, 1967

[38]   PIAGET, J. *The Child's Conception of Physical Causality*, Routledge & Kegan Paul, 1930

[39]   PIAGET, J., *The Moral Judgment of the Child*, Routledge & Kegan Paul, 1932

[40]   PIAGET, J., *The Psychology of Intelligence*, Routledge & Kegan Paul, 1947

[41]   PIAGET, J., *The Child's Conception of Number*, Routledge & Kegan Paul, 1952

[42] PIAGET, J., *Play, Dreams and Imitation in Childhood*, Routledge & Kegan Paul, 1962

[43] PIAGET, J., *The Child's Construction of Reality*, Routledge & Kegan Paul, 1955

[44] PIAGET, J. and INHELDER, B., *The Child's Conception of Space*, Routledge & Kegan Paul, 1963

[45] POPPER, K., *Conjectures and Refutations*, 2nd ed. (rev.), Routledge & Kegan Paul, 1965

[46] READ, Sir H., *Education through Art*, Faber, 1961

[47] ROSENBLITH, J. F. and ALLINSMITH, W., *The Causes of Behaviour II*, Boston, Allyn & Bacon, 1966

[48] SCHOOLS COUNCIL, *Mathematics in Primary Schools*, H.M.S.O., 1966

[49] SIMPSON, D. and ALDERSON, D. M., *Creative Play in the Infants' School*, Pitman, 1950

[50] TOULMIN, S., *Foresight and Understanding*, Hutchinson, 1961

[51] VYGOTSKY, L. S., *Thought and Language*, New York, Wiley, 1962

[52] WILSON, J., WILLIAMS, N. and SUGARMAN, B., *Introduction to Moral Education*, Harmondsworth, Penguin Books, 1967

Glossary

Accommodation An elaboration or modification of schemata to meet variations in experience, resulting in a higher level of understanding or a more appropriate response.

Assimilation The cumulative incorporation of experience without modification into existing schemata (q.v.) (see also *Accommodation*).

Affective A general term used in psychology to refer to processes concerned with feeling and emotion, as distinct from cognitive (q.v.).

Cognitive A general term used in psychology to refer to processes involved in knowing, e.g. perception, remembering, imagining, judging and reasoning.

Concept A general idea organized from previous experience through which certain events or objects are understood to have common attributes or relationships and therefore to constitute a category. Concepts thus act as frames of reference for subsequent behaviour.

Conservation The formation of ideas which are constant and permanent even in the face of perceptual transformations.

Egocentric The characteristic of judging or interpreting from one's own point of view. It is used to describe a stage in development when children are intellectually unable to put themselves at a point of view other than their own.

Genetic Psychology An explanation of human psychological development in terms of progressive stages of growth from simple sensory-motor actions to complex thinking operations, brought about by continuous interaction between a person and the world around him.

Heuristic Heuristic procedures are those in which the material is presented in such a way that it involves practical investigation appropriate to the form of knowledge concerned, and where the learner comes to discover principles for himself.

Kinesphere The space surrounding each individual, the natural boundaries of which are determined by the normal reach of the limbs.

188

Operational Mental activity not dominated by perception and imagery. It is characterized by the ability to hold in mind the relationships within a situation and leads to thinking which conforms to logical criteria.

Percept The immediate awareness of something through any of the senses.

Perseveration A term used in psychology to refer to the tendency for a response (action, idea or feeling) associated with a previous experience to recur without modification.

Pre-operational Describes mental activity which is dominated by perception and imagery and which can prevent the structuring of consistent and realistic ideas.

Representation The processes by which past experience is mentally conserved to enable reference to objects and events no longer present to the senses.

Reversibility The ability to trace and retrace the steps in thought between the end and the beginning of an idea.

Schema A generalized repeatable pattern of behaviour or thought organized from past experience and actively ready to assimilate new experience.

Sensory Motor A term used to describe exploration through the senses or through manipulation. There is a stage in development from birth to approximately eighteen months to two years when only this type of exploration and understanding is available.

Spatial Orientation The awareness of the relationship of the body to different divisions of space.

Vertical Grouping A form of school organization in which the ages of the children in each group cover several years.

Index